CHRIST IN ME

FIGHTING THE STUBBORN SINS

J. DANIEL BODE

WESTBOW
PRESS*
A DIVISION OF THOMAS NELSON
& ZONDERVAN

Scripture taken from the King James Version of the Bible.

WestBow Press books may be ordered through booksellers or by contacting:

WestBow Press
A Division of Thomas Nelson & Zondervan
1663 Liberty Drive
Bloomington, IN 47403
www.westbowpress.com
1 (866) 928-1240

ISBN: 978-1-9736-2319-9 (sc)
ISBN: 978-1-9736-2320-5 (e)

Library of Congress Control Number: 2018903332

Print information available on the last page.

WestBow Press rev. date: 03/27/2018

ACKNOWLEDGEMENTS

I grew up in a Christian family that went to church every time the doors were open, and was saved at a young age, and cannot tell you the date. But I remember distinctly where I was, and asking the Lord Jesus Christ to forgive me of my sins and be my Lord and Savior. I was at my Grandmother's house, and we had been talking about God and His love for me, and His desire to bring me into a personal relationship with Him

I wish I could say that I followed Him from that day forward, but this is not the case. Not long after being saved, I felt the call to be a missionary, and gladly accepted it. But, in my teenage years, I started a long journey away from God and His love. I became addicted to alcohol by the age of twenty-two, after dropping out of Tennessee Temple University, where I had gone to learn to preach. I spent the next eight years of my life running from God and anything having to do with religion.

God let me run from Him and get myself deeper and deeper into a sinful lifestyle until my wife and I finally separated and filed for divorce in 2008. By His mercy and grace, He stopped this from happening, and restored my family. This is when I finally got back into church, and God brought men into my life that encouraged me in my walk with Him. God renewed my call into the ministry, and has put my terrible past to use in the ministry in which I serve.

Because of my past of addiction, God is using my wife and I in recovery ministry and discipleship. I will never say that He led me to the life I lived, but I will certainly say that He is fully capable of using my ragged past for His glory and honor! Because I come from a life of addiction, I am well-schooled in what it takes to come out of this lifestyle. God is opening doors of opportunity for us to preach to and train others that are looking for a better life, away from these things. I believe my call to missions is directly from God, and He has given me a burden to work with church members, addicts and inmates, teaching them about the love of Christ, and about the Way to true freedom.

The devotions in this book are written with a prayer that God will use them in the life of the reader. God has the power to take a broken life and make something beautiful out of it. God has the power to turn your fears into strengths, and to turn your failures into victories. God has reached out His loving hand to every person who has ever lived upon this earth, offering to take their sins, faults, and failures upon Himself. There is no way that any one of us could ever meet the requirements of a just, holy, and righteous God, and so He made a way for us to know Him. That way is through the pages of Scripture, and through the life of Jesus Christ.

God wants to have a personal relationship with you, the object of His love, mercy, and grace. He offers this relationship to each of us, free to us. This relationship is one that can change your life, and your world. If you have never experienced the life changing love of God personally, I invite you to begin it today. 2 Corinthians 6:2 says, "For He saith, I have heard thee in a time accepted, and in the day of salvation have I succoured thee: behold, now is the accepted time; behold, now is the day of salvation." If you have never placed your faith in Jesus Christ, He is waiting on you this minute.

The path to salvation is the first path one must follow in order to have a victorious life over sin and addiction. There are a few things you must understand in order to begin your Christian life:

1. Romans 3:23, "For all have sinned, and come short of the glory of God."

    There is no person alive today who has not sinned. We each have to acknowledge the fact that if we stand before God with only our righteousness, we will fall far short of what He demands of us.

2. Romans 6:23, "For the wages of sin is death, but the gift of God is eternal life, through Jesus Christ our Lord."

    When we work, we earn a pay check, or a wage. Because of our sin, the Bible tells us that our wage is eternal separation from God. This is as good as we can earn with anything that we do. But God has given us a gift of eternal life, and this gift has come through Jesus Christ.

3. Romans 5:8, "But God commendeth His love toward us, in that, while we were yet sinners, Christ died for us."

    The gift offered by God came at a great cost to Him: the death of His Son. He loved us so much that He was willing to let His Son be put to death.

4. Romans 10:9-10, "That if thou shalt confess with thy mouth the Lord Jesus, and shalt believe in thine heart that God hath raised him from the dead, thou shalt be saved. For with the heart man believeth unto righteousness; and with the mouth confession is made unto salvation."

    The gift offered by God is free to us, but not forced upon us. If someone hands you a present, you must reach out your hand and accept it, or reject it. The way to accept this gift is to confess, or agree with God, that you are a sinner, and fall short of His demands. You must choose to place your faith upon the work that Jesus Christ did upon the Cross.

5. Romans 10:13, "For whosoever calleth upon the name of the Lord shall be saved."

    This is the best promise that you and I have ever heard. It is a guarantee of God's grace and mercy in our lives, for eternity!

Friend, I pray that if you have not looked to Jesus for the saving of your eternal soul, that you will do so this minute. He offers you a chance of forgiveness and acceptance today. This offer is not guaranteed to be there for you tomorrow.

No matter if you are a new Christian, or have been a Christian for many years; no matter if you are struggling to overcome strongholds and addictions in your life, or you are seeking to help someone overcome theirs, the wisdom you need can be found in the Word of God. This book is not meant to be a substitute for Scripture, but to help the reader better understand what Scripture is saying.

BLESSED IS THE MAN

Psalms 1:1-2, "Blessed is the man that walketh not after the counsel of the ungodly, nor standeth in the way of sinners, nor sitteth in the seat of the scornful. But his delight is in the law of the LORD; and in His law doth he meditate day and night."

There are many ideas in the world today about what it means to be blessed. Many will tell us that great riches are the way to blessing, and also proof that one has been blessed. It is with this idea that many go to great, and often, illegal lengths to gain great wealth. Many families have been broken, and many lives completely destroyed in this way. But as we look into the lives of some of the very wealthy people we know, many times we can find only loneliness and emptiness after they have achieved their lofty goals. Surely this is not what it means to be blessed.

Some will tell us that great fame is the proof of being blessed. It doesn't really matter how you get famous, as long as everyone knows your name. Again, many of the celebrities we know about leave behind them a terrible trail of broken hearts, families, and promises. We can see a quickly growing number of people in jails and prisons today who have spent their time trying to make a name for themselves for all the wrong reasons. Again, this cannot be the way to blessing.

In these verses lies the key to being a person that is greatly blessed; because they are blessed by the Lord. The first qualification is that one does not follow ungodly counsel. God is the standard by which all things are judged good or bad. The Bible tells us in James 1:17, "Every good gift and every perfect gift is from above, and cometh down from the Father of lights, with whom is no variableness, neither shadow of turning." If we want to be truly blessed, we must follow godly counsel!

The second qualification is that we do not live in the same fashion as the unsaved and ungodly. Remembering that the first qualification is not to follow ungodly counsel, we will live our lives differently from those who would give it. To "stand in the way of sinners" is to conform to their world view. Instead, the Bible tells us in Romans 12:2, "And be not conformed to this world: but be ye transformed by the renewing of your mind, that ye may prove what is that good, and acceptable, and perfect, will of God." To be truly blessed by God, we must have a mind that has been transformed by the Word of God. This requires study and meditation of Scriptures.

The third qualification is that we do not sit in the seat of the scornful. This means to "dwell in the seat of a judge." We all know people who judge the actions and intents of everyone around them. We also all know someone who looks at every Christian and passes judgment on them just for the fact that they say they are Christians. These people are simply looking for reasons to hate others. Instead, we should live a life of love towards those around us. 1 Corinthians 13:4-8 tells us that love is long suffering, kind, and humble, does not envy others, seeks to help others, and is always present.

Finally, the person most blessed by God is one who delights in God's Law, and meditates in it constantly. If we want the blessing of God upon our lives, we must know what pleases and displeases Him. We must know what He likes, and what He hates. We must know how He wants us to treat others. We must know what He expects of us. Simply put, we must know the mind of God. This is impossible to do without much study of His Law. Many excuses can be given why one does not have time to spend in God's Word and God's work. Everyone today is busy. But we always make time to do the things we love to do; those things that give us pleasure.

All of us would like to be blessed. The question is, do we want it bad enough to follow God to true blessing and purpose in our lives?

STRENGTH FROM GOD

Psalms 1:3, "And he shall be like a tree planted by the rivers of water, that bringeth forth his fruit in his season; his leaf also shall not wither; and whatsoever he doeth shall prosper."

We have probably all seen trees that were planted in a dry area, or an area that has become dry since the planting of a tree. These trees are often brittle, finding barely enough nourishment to survive. They are smaller than well watered trees, and often very ugly. Without fail, they will never live as long as a healthy, well watered tree.

Taking this description and applying it to a person, we see a frail individual, spending everything he has just on the bare necessities of life; and often not getting enough of even the bare necessities. We see a person who has put their faith in the world system; lying paths marked as going to success. There are many of these paths in life. They start out filled with fun and good times, but end by destroying the person, their family, and any hope for change.

But what a promise we find here! In this verse, we learn what will happen when we follow verses one and two. The outcome of using godly counsel, walking among the righteous, and living a life of love towards those around us instead of being judgmental, is something we all long for! This person will be like a tree planted by rivers of water.

A tree planted in well watered ground has a jump start on a vibrant and long life. The roots do not have to search hard for water and nourishment; everything pertaining to life is right there! This gives it a chance to grow; and it grows fast, tall, and strong! As the tree grows in height, the roots also dig deeper and wider, providing strength against the storms that the tree will undoubtedly encounter. The soil was soft enough to allow the root system to get a good start, and soon, the system has found the harder ground it needs for strength, while still having access to the good ground with the essentials for life.

This can be a great picture of our life—if we will follow God with our whole heart. He is the well watered ground. He is the nourishment we need. He is the harder ground that gives us strength to get through the storms of life. The more we know Him, the more we grow! The more we study Him, the deeper and wider our root system grows, providing yet more strength and faith.

Next, we see the fruit of this tree. It is never questioned if the tree will bear fruit or not. No matter how dry the year is, the tree planted by the river will give bountifully! This is the life of a strong Christian who seeks to follow God! No matter how bad things get in our lives, God promises that our life will be fruitful; fruitful in the Christian life, as well as our personal life, because we are drawing our needs from the One who created us.

The verse goes on to say that this trees leaf shall not wither. The tree that goes without water, even in the height of the growing season, often loses its leaves very early in the year. The people planted in the dry, unnourishing soil of life will soon experience their dreams and hopes come crashing down. Their goals in life will many times go unfulfilled. But the person who puts his trust in God will have growth not only in the growing season, but also in the dormant season!

Finally, we see this person is blessed of the Lord for living the life of faith so much that everything he does will be prospered by the Lord. This is not to say that we will never stumble and fall; it simply means that God will always be there to pick us up. God can use even the terrible times of our lives to grow us; even our failures can be used by Him to make us what He wants us to be.

GODLY, OR GOD-LESS

Psalm 1:4-5, "The ungodly are not so: but are like the chaff which the wind driveth away. Therefore the ungodly shall not stand in the judgment, nor sinners in the congregation of the righteous."

We have seen in verses 1-3 the benefits of being a person who seeks to please the Lord. They tell us that if we put our delight in Him, and meditate daily upon His Word, that He will bless us. He will make everything we do to prosper. Now, let's look at the person who does contrary to His Law.

Everything that God promises will happen for the righteous person, He also promises will not happen to the unrighteous person. Instead of being a tree planted by rivers of water, growing and vibrant, with deep roots that give strength to make it through the storms of life, he will be a withered up and dying tree. He will have no strength to stand through the storms of life. At the first sign of trouble or temptation he will crumble.

Everyone wants to have a good life. There is not one person on this planet that started out with the intentions of becoming addicted to anything. Those of us who have been in addiction, or are currently in addiction will tell anyone who cares to know that this is not how they envisioned their life. It all started out as fun and games, and before you knew it, it was unstoppable. This is simply because you have followed the path contrary to the one that will bring blessing from God. This verse has come true in your life, and as you look, you may not see a way out. Friend, as the tree dries up, it becomes harder and harder to bring it to a point where it can take nourishment once again, and become healthy. The verse explains it farther by saying that the ungodly are like the chaff that the wind drives away. The chaff is the stem that a head of wheat sits on top of. In harvesting time, they would cut the whole stem down, take it to the threshing floor, beat the wheat off of it, then throw everything up in the air. The wheat, being heavy, fell back to the floor, while the chaff blew away. This ungodly person is like the chaff—there is nothing of substance in him; even the smallest wind can blow him off course. This is what has happened! You may want to do good; you want to do right; but the smallest thing comes into your life and blows you off course again and again.

The next verse tells what the final outcome of this man will be. He will not be able to stand in the time of judgment. Judgment at the end of life is something the devil doesn't want you to think about. He will keep sending those winds of pleasure into your life to keep you going off track. But don't be fooled; each of us will stand one day before our creator, and give account of our lives. If you have lived your life on the wrong side of verses 1-3, you will find yourself at the end of verse 5; you will not be able to stand.

The Law we will be judged by is a Law that no one can follow in their own power. If we look to ourselves to please God, we will fail every time! But He promises help; if we delight ourselves in His Law. He will do through us what we cannot do on our own. We simple have to put our trust in Him. He knows we will not—cannot be perfect, and so He offers us the help we so desperately need. It is there for anyone who will take it through faith! Make no mistake; you will stumble sometimes. You may even fall from time to time. The road to a life of true freedom must be travelled one day at a time; one step at a time. But it is a road that the Lord can and will help us travel if we delight ourselves in Him.

One last thought; it is a journey that, like all others, must start with the first step. It is a war that must begin with the first battle. As you take the first step, and then another, and another, God will begin working in your life, bringing true life back into the withered tree. With each step, He will make you stronger. Why not start the journey today?

THE ONE WHO KNOWS

Psalm 1:6, "For the Lord knoweth the way of the righteous, but the way of the ungodly shall perish."

If we were to be honest about it, there is probably not one of us that at some point in our new walk with Jesus Christ that has not looked out on the world, seeing all the evil that prospers, and thought to ourselves that what we are trying to do doesn't make sense. Those who are doing evil are getting by with it, and living a good life on this earth, while most Christians are barely getting by. We love God, and give our time, money, and work to the church for free, while they love themselves, and make money while living for the next dollar.

There is only one problem with this way of thinking: God knows the truth about everyone, and He will be everyone's final judge. We see today, but God sees years in advance. We see only what is on the outside, but God sees the inside. We see the fun and games in their lives, but God sees the emptiness and turmoil that follows them around everywhere they go.

There are many who think they are getting away with the evil they do, and the harm they do to others. While we may not understand why the Lord lets things go on like they do, we have to come to the understanding that He has given every person a free will to do as they choose, even if it means they choose to hurt others by serving themselves.

While it is true that we lost many "friends" when God changed our lives, we have gained so much more in Him and Him alone. If He is the only friend we have until the day we die, we have more than the wealthiest sinner that has ever walked the earth. Because we have made the decision to let Jesus be Lord of our lives in the present, He has made the decision to honor us with eternal life in the future. Make no mistake; we will all answer to the same God, sooner or later.

God has given us the promise that He will provide the things we need if we follow Him. Jesus tells us in Matthew 11:28-29, "Come unto me, all ye that labour and are heavy laden, and I will give you rest. Take my yoke upon you, and learn of me; for I am meek and lowly in heart: and ye shall find rest unto your souls." Don't let the enemy draw you away from the protection of the Lord by filling your eyes with the easy life of the world around you. It is just an illusion!

He also has a promise, and a warning for those who would reject Him. Romans 14:11, "For it is written, as I live, sayeth the Lord, every knee shall bow to me, and every tongue shall confess to God." God gives each person a chance to choose or reject Him in this life, but there will come a day when even those who hate Him shall bow to Him, and confess that He is the rightful God.

I don't know your heart, but you can be assured that God does. Our verse tells us that God knows the way (the walk, as well as the final destination) of the righteous, and goes on to say that the way of the ungodly shall perish. Have you come to a time in your life that you have willingly come to Him, asking forgiveness for your sins? Have you given Him the control of your life? If not, He is giving you that opportunity right now. He will not force you to choose Him; but He longs for you to come to Him. 2 Peter 3:9, "The Lord is not slack concerning His promise, as some men count slackness; but is longsuffering to us-ward, not willing that any should perish, but that all should come to repentance."

There is no person that loves you like God does. There is no person who would, or has, given you the things that God has. He is calling you now to come to Him in faith. Come, before it is eternally too late.

SPIRITUAL FRUIT AND ITS BENEFITS

Galatians 5:22-23, "But the fruit of the Spirit is love, joy, peace, longsuffering, gentleness, goodness, faith, meekness, temperance: against such there is no law."

After a non-believer comes into a relationship with Jesus Christ, God's plan is that there are there are several things that will change in his life. A life that was once lived in chaos, God wants to fill with peace and contentment. A life that was once consumed with self-desire, God wants to turn into a life that is consumed by love towards Him, and a desire to live a God honoring life that will lead others to faith in Christ. A life that was once in bondage to sin and addiction, God wants to turn into a life that is filled with freedom from the bondage of sin.

As with all things in our Christian walk, we have a lot to say about if God will be able to do those things with our lives that He wants to do. We can choose to live for Him, giving Him glory and honor through our lives, or we can choose to remain self-centered and ignore God's plans for us. God will never force you and I to serve Him, but if we choose to live for ourselves after our salvation experience, we can be sure of either one of these two things: either our salvation experience was a fake, and we have never truly been saved, or we will live the rest of our lives in misery. While God will never force the Christian to serve Him, He will certainly chastise him for refusing to live the way he should live.

We know, from reading other passages in Scripture, that as Christians, we can turn back into our old lifestyle. One such passage can be found in Galatians 4:9, "But now, after that ye have known God, or rather are known of God, how turn ye again to the weak and beggarly elements, whereunto ye desire again to be in bondage?" The Galatians Paul was writing to had truly known the life changing experience of salvation. They had been saved, and had been brought by God out of the bondage they were in by sin. But they had chosen to go back to their old ways.

The Christian who lives his life for Christ will find that it is a hard life to live. The sins you and I have battled with will many times be found knocking on our heart's door, trying to find a way to sneak back into our lives, placing us, once again, in bondage. These sins will come knocking in the form of friends and family. They will come knocking with fond memories of the past, and also with terrible memories. They will try to pry our heart's door open when we have a bad day at work, or when we receive terrible news. And they will try to fool us into believing that we can get away with indulging in some "small sin" just once, or by allowing ourselves to retain some habit that we know God is not pleased with.

Due to all of these ways we can find ourselves falling back into the bondage of sin and addiction, it is clear that we need spiritual help and guidance. God is pleased to offer this help in the form of the Holy Spirit. The Holy Spirit is here to help us, and guide us. We are told in Ephesians 5:18, "And be not drunk with wine, wherein is excess; but be filled with the Spirit." This verse lets us understand that being filled with the Spirit is a choice we make, not something that automatically happens at some point in our lives. We choose, every day, whether we will spend the day filled with the Spirit, or filled with ourselves.

We can only be filled with the Spirit as we read, study, and meditate upon Scripture, and as we submit to His leading in our lives. When we are faced with temptation, if we choose to follow that temptation, we are refusing to let the Spirit have His way in our lives; if we turn from that temptation, and do what we know God wants us to do, we are following the Spirit. God will put in our hearts, the desire to do things for Him, through the Spirit. When we choose to follow His prompts, and do things that honor and glorify Him, we are submitting to Him.

As we spend more and more time studying, meditating, and submitting to Him, we will find that our lives begin to change in a fundamental way. Our sinful desires will begin to be smaller, and have less power. Our ability to follow and obey Him will increase. And our personality will begin to change. This is because of the fruit of the Spirit growing in our hearts and lives. For the next several days, we are going to discuss this fruit. It is something that can only come through submitting to the Holy Spirit. This fruit cannot be produced by us, but it is produced by the Holy Spirit, in us. If we will allow Him to plant, and grow, this fruit in our lives, it will change everything about our lives. Will you commit today to allow the Spirit to have His way in your life? If so, you will never regret it!

FRUITS OF THE SPIRIT: LOVE

Galatians 5:22-23, "But the fruit of the Spirit is love, joy, peace, longsuffering, gentleness, goodness, faith, meekness, temperance: against such there is no law."

The first fruit of the Spirit that is mentioned, and the one fruit upon which all the other fruits are dependent upon is love. Without having love in our lives, we will never know the other eight fruits listed in this verse. This fruit is the most known fruit of the Spirit, and also the most misunderstood and misused. Everyone uses the word love, but there are very few people who truly understand what it is. Many think that because we love others, we must let them do wrong, and some would say that because God loves us, we can do anything we want, and He will look the other way; nothing could be farther from the truth.

As Christians, we must first understand what this word truly means. 2 John 1:6 gives us the meaning of what our love for the Lord will bring about in our lives; "And this is love, that we walk after His commandments. This is the commandment, that, as ye have heard from the beginning, ye should walk in it." In our natural state, we could never love God. On the contrary, the unconverted person hates God. He hates God because God has a standard that he can never reach. He hates God because God demands obedience to His Law. Even after a true salvation experience, the heart of a person is changed, but the flesh is still the same, longing after the sins and pleasures this world offers. But upon salvation, God gives us the power to have victory over the flesh, and its sinful desires. We each have a choice on a daily basis, whether we will choose to love God, and walk after His commandments, or whether we will love the flesh, and walk after the fulfillment of its demands. Before salvation, we fought a hopeless battle against our sinful desires, but when God granted us salvation, He also gave us the ability to love Him.

Along with the ability to love God comes a new ability to love others. 1 John 4: 7-8, "Beloved, let us love one another: for love is of God; and every one that loveth is born of God, and knoweth God. He that loveth not knoweth not God; for God is love." The world thinks that love is a feeling. People get married because they feel affection for someone, but soon that affection gives way to aggravation and disgust. This is why we see so much divorce today. These feelings will never remain the same. Relationships must be built upon something more stable than our feelings, whether they are marriage relationships, or friendships. This love that God gives us the ability to have is the foundation that any relationship must be built upon, if it is to stand the test of time. We are given a command in this verse to love one another. In the previous paragraph, we found out what God's definition of love towards Him is, and that is following His commands. To love Him is to glorify Him. The same is true of the love we have for others. It has nothing to do with feelings, but everything to do with holding others up, or glorifying them. God gives us the ability, through the power of the Holy Spirit, to love others, holding them up, even if those same people do not show us love, another command that we are given in Luke 6:35.

1 Corinthians 13 is known as the great love chapter in the Bible. Here's what verses 4-8 have to say about love; "Charity (love) suffereth long, and is kind; charity envieth not; charity vaunteth not

itself, is not puffed up, doth not behave itself unseemly, seeketh not her own, is not easily provoked, thinketh no evil; rejoiceth not in iniquity, but rejoiceth in the truth; beareth all things, believeth all things, hopeth all things, endureth all things. Charity never faileth…." As we read these verses, it becomes very clear to us that we could never display God's kind of love in our own power. How is it possible to love someone this way when they hurt you physically, or emotionally? How is it possible to love someone this way when everything they do has a negative effect upon your life? There is a very final answer to these questions. It is impossible for us to love like we should love in our own power. But God gives us the Holy Spirit, who will guide us, and give us the strength to carry out God's commands.

This power cannot be found inside us. We cannot love God, or our friends and family, in our own strength. But if we will allow God to have His way in our hearts, He will grow this fruit. He does not need our help, only our willingness to give Him access and influence in our lives. To be sure, we will not see this growth complete all at once, but if we will commit our hearts to Him, He will begin to grow a wonderful garden inside us, and the results will be constant, and more prominent in our lives as we continue to submit to the Spirit's leading.

FRUITS OF THE SPIRIT: JOY

Galatians 5:22-23, "But the fruit of the Spirit is love, joy, peace, longsuffering, gentleness, goodness, faith, meekness, temperance: against such there is no law."

The second fruit mentioned in this verse is joy. There is not a person who has ever lived who did not seek to have a life of joy. Many have searched for the fulfillment of joy by having a position of power. Some seek joy from great wealth, and spend a lifetime trying to make their fortune. Some seek joy from a simple life, refusing to get caught up in the chaos of life. Still others think that joy can be found in a marriage union. The one thing that each of these types of people have in common is that once they have achieved their goals, they find that joy has eluded them.

All of the things mentioned here have a place in a well-rounded life, but these things alone will never provide the joy we seek, and need, for a healthy life. We must first understand what joy is, and then know what can bring it. The world has fallen for the deadly lie that happiness is joy, and so it lives day after day pursuing the things that give happiness, instead of pursuing the things that can give joy. Happiness comes and goes, dictated by the pleasures and stresses that we face every day. The happiness provided by a success today will quickly fade away when we are faced with a failure tomorrow. True joy will remain in our hearts, even when we are struggling through our failures, or the failures of others. True joy is a cheerful, calm delight and rejoicing in a particular circumstance. This joy is priceless, and will carry us through the many times in life that we find it impossible to be happy. This joy will keep us from going back to our former lifestyle when we are attacked by the enemy!

Ecclesiastes chapter 3 talks about there being a time for everything, including a time to weep, and a time to hate. James 1:2 tells us to count it all joy when we fall into temptations, or trials. If the Lord's definition of joy were what most people think of joy being, then the Bible would be contradicting itself; there is no possible way we can be happy when faced with these kinds of conditions. We must understand that joy does not come from the worldly things that we have spent much of our lives pursuing!

True joy can only come from one source; our Creator. As we keep our lives and hearts in submission to God's plan for us, He provides this joy through the Holy Spirit. We hold the key for this Fruit of the Spirit to grow within us, and that key is our obedience to God's Word. It is through this joy we can possess in the trials of life that the world around us will see Christ in us. It is because of this joy that we can keep serving the Lord when everything is falling apart around us. As we spend more and more time in submission to His leading, we will find our joy becoming bigger and more powerful in our lives. The more we submit to Him, the more joy we will have!

The reason this fruit is so very important in the believer's life is that it will keep us working for Him when times are hard, and keep us walking in the path He has led us to, even when the path is straight uphill. This joy that comes from the Holy Spirit tells us that everything we are going through today will be worth it when we reach tomorrow. It reminds us that God is in control even when our world is out of control. It tells us that God is allowing the evil that we face because it will bring about His glory and honor.

It is this joy that Jesus Christ experienced throughout His lifetime, being in perfect submission to the Father. It is this joy that allowed Him to walk in the midst of men who hated Him, and plotted His death. It is this joy that even went with Him as He carried His own cross up to the place where He would be nailed upon it, and die for the sins of the world.

It is this same joy that God wants you to have in this life. Because of it, you will be able to withstand anything your enemy throws at you, because you will understand that God has allowed it for His own purposes, and that He is in complete control. This joy will make you understand that you are not living for today, but for an eternity of tomorrows with your Savior. It will help you face what you must endure today with a cheerful, calm delight, because God is in control of your circumstances.

It is only through obedience and submission to God that this Fruit will grow in us, but disobedience will take it away. In Psalm 51:12-13, we find King David asking God to restore the joy of salvation to him. David prayed this prayer after his sin was revealed to him by the Prophet Nathan. David had been living with unconfessed sin in his life, and he was living in misery. As David confessed his sin, God brought joy to him once again, and continued to use David in mighty ways.

Have you been caught up in seeking happiness instead of joy? Have you found that you can only have limited victory over the sins you battle, finding that you constantly fall back when the pressures of life hit you hard, making you unhappy? Why not try to pursue God, instead of happiness? If you will, He will give you a joy that supersedes any happiness you have ever encountered.

FRUITS OF THE SPIRIT: PEACE

Galatians 5:22-23, "But the fruit of the Spirit is love, joy, peace, longsuffering, gentleness, goodness, faith, meekness, temperance: against such there is no law."

The third Fruit of the Spirit is peace. Peace is something that mankind has searched for ever since his horrific fall taken in the Garden of Eden. He searches for peace in his heart, and for peace with others in the world in which he lives. He seeks peace at his place of employment, and with his family when he arrives home.

Ever since sin has entered into the hearts of men and women, Satan has been there telling lies about the things that give peace. Many have fallen for the lie that this peace can be found in drugs and alcohol. Some seek peace by withdrawing themselves from others. Many others think it can be found in religion. One thing is certain; at the end of the search for peace in any of the avenues offered by the world, only chaos and bondage will be found.

True peace can only be found in Jesus Christ. The peace He offers will be with us in the calm, as well as the storm. It tells that we can truly rest in the times when things are going well, not worrying about the trouble we may see on the horizon, because we have a Savior who is strong enough to see us through this trouble. It reminds us that we can put complete trust in Him when we are going through the storms that were on the horizon yesterday.

Psalm 119:165, "Great peace have they which love thy law: and nothing shall offend them." As with all the other Fruits of the Spirit, this peace is given through the Holy Spirit. What we do with it is up to us. This verse gives the secret to having great and powerful peace in our lives. It says, simply, that if we love God's Law, then we will have great peace. It tells us that although the world may be against us, we can never be destroyed by it. As we come closer to our Lord, the ability to have peace in our lives will grow. As we study and meditate upon the Word of God, letting it change us, we will experience more peace.

We can read much in Scripture about the peace that is provided for the believer. Psalm 55:22, "Cast thy burden upon the Lord, and He shall sustain thee: He shall never suffer the righteous to be moved." God offers us a chance to give Him our burdens, no matter what they are. His promise to us is that not only will He take our burdens, but He will sustain us, providing everything that we need. This world wants to see the Christian stumble and fall; its desire is to drive the Christian to his knees, through any means possible. Oh, the wonderful knowledge that we serve a God who is all powerful, able to take the struggles and problems we have, while at the same time providing anything we need, both physically and spiritually! We can have perfect peace, in all areas of life, because we know, and serve, a God who has all strength and power!

We often try to get through this life and its problems in our own strength. Jesus tells us in Matthew 11:28, "Come unto me, all who are weary and heavy laden, and I will give you rest." Jesus Christ knows very well how taxing this world can be on us. He knows from personal experience the problems and enemies we face. He offers every person a chance to give every problem, every burden, to Him, and let Him carry if for us. Why do we so often ignore this gracious offer, trying to carry the crushing weight of the world by ourselves? We can never expect to make it through this life on our own. He offers this wonderful fruit to us, so that we can tell Him our problems, and trust that He will take care of them.

Matthew 11:29, "Take my yoke upon you, and learn of me; for I am meek and lowly in heart: and ye shall find rest unto your souls." Taking yoke of Jesus is allowing Him to be our Prophet, Priest, and King. Jesus wants to be our Savior, and our Lord. If we are willing to allow Him this, He promises us this wonderful fruit in our hearts. Are you tired of struggling to carry the crushing burdens of life that are much too heavy for you to bear? Have you caught yourself thinking of how much you would be willing to pay for just a few hours of peace? Jesus offers this peace, free of charge to you. Not only that, but He offers to carry your burdens as well.

FRUITS OF THE SPIRIT: LONGSUFFERING

Galatians 5:22-23, "But the fruit of the Spirit is love, joy, peace, longsuffering, gentleness, goodness, faith, meekness, temperance: against such there is no law."

The next fruit of the Spirit is longsuffering, or patience. This is something that is greatly lacking in our world today, and in the lives of many Christians as well. We live in a time in which we have become accustomed to having the things we want immediately, with no waiting at all. We have fast food, fast cars, convenience stores, microwave popcorn, and in many churches, fifteen minute sermons. There are countless companies that advertise "just in time service." We have been led to believe that if something takes longer than we like it to, it is not something we want, and as soon as someone does something we do not like, we feel justified in dismissing them as a friend.

The word patience is not a word most of us like to talk about; but it is a word that we need to know about, and an asset that all of us need to have. Being a fruit of the Spirit, we each have the seed within us, waiting for the soil of our hearts to workable enough for the Holy Spirit to grow it. Without this fruit thriving in the heart of a weak Christian, or an addict, it will be impossible for us to overcome the things we struggle with. Without a strong Christian actively working to keep his heart workable to the Holy Spirit, he will quickly find himself becoming weaker.

As with all the other fruits of the Spirit, this fruit is available to us upon salvation, but it also must be nourished and allowed to grow. The Christian cannot be victorious in the Christian walk without it! Without it, we will find ourselves falling back into our past lifestyles time after time. Without it, we will find ourselves without friends, or family, to help us in our walk. In short, without it we will have lonely lives filled with defeat and failure. Having patience will allow us to face discouragement with a positive attitude, instead of letting that discouragement drag us back down into what we are trying to come out of. We can see a perfect example from Jesus, in the way He dealt with others throughout His lifetime. He showed patience and love to everyone He ever met.

The discouragement we often face in life is so devastating to us, mostly because we forget God's promises to help us. When faced with the failure of a friend or loved one, we often only see the immediate effects upon us caused by their failure. As we think about these things, we put ourselves in great danger of falling back into the things that God has pulled us from. Instead of focusing on these things, the Lord reminds us in numerous passages of Scripture that He is in complete control, and that He will never fail in His promises to us. He wants to make us better, stronger Christians through these problems, as well as use us to encourage those around us. When we are faced with these discouragements, we choose to either have patience, trusting God is in control, or to ignore God, and focus on our problems.

2 Peter 3:9, "The Lord is not slack concerning His promise, as some men count slackness; but is longsuffering to us-ward, not willing that any should perish, but that all should come to repentance." The Lord shows us longsuffering time after time when we fail Him, forget Him, and ignore Him. Many times we think He allows us to get away with our sins, when in fact, He

is just displaying patience with us. Many of us could give testimony to years that we spent in sin, with God displaying His beautiful patience towards us, all the time leading us to the point in our lives that we would turn ourselves over to His leadership. This is what He wants from us as well; for us to display this patience towards others in our lives, showing them love in return for their wrongdoing.

The road to great patience is hard, but very rewarding to us, both physically and spiritually. When you make the decision to walk down this road, your enemy will hit you hard, trying to discourage you, using situations, friends, and family to stop your journey. But God is powerful, and is able to turn these very situations around for your benefit, if only you will keep going. James 1:3, "Knowing this, that the trying of your faith worketh patience." If God never allowed Satan to attack you, this fruit would never grow. This is God's purpose in allowing you to face these times in life.

James 1:4, "But let patience have her perfect work, that ye may be perfect and entire, wanting nothing." This is God's promise to you. If you will allow Him to lead you, He will indeed lead you through some rough paths; but they will be engineered to use the things your enemy wants to destroy you with to make you a stronger Christian instead.

Are you allowing the Holy Spirit to use your discouragements to create a heart full of patience, or are you letting Satan use these things to drag you back into a life of misery, for you, as well as everyone who loves you?

FRUITS OF THE SPIRIT: GENTLENESS

Galatians 5:22-23, "But the fruit of the Spirit is love, joy, peace, longsuffering, gentleness, goodness, faith, meekness, temperance: against such there is no law."

The next Fruit of the Spirit we see in this verse is the Fruit of gentleness. The thought that we can have gentleness flowing from us is almost unreal as we think about dealing with a world that has gone crazy. But as we begin to cooperate with the Holy Spirit, letting Him direct us, this is exactly what can happen. We can have gentleness in a world that loves harshness, violence and hatefulness.

We are told in Ephesians 4:31-32, "Let all bitterness, and wrath, and anger, and clamour, and evil speaking, be put away from you, will all malice: and be ye kind one to another, tenderhearted, forgiving one another, even as God for Christ's sake hath forgiven you." If we want the seed of gentleness that has been planted in our hearts by the Holy Spirit to grow, there are things we must do to make our hearts fertile ground. The things we are given in these verses to avoid are where our enemy can sneak in, destroying the good fruit that God wants to grow into our lives. If we are to follow the instructions given here, it will never be something we do in our own power; we must be submissive to the Holy Spirit's leading.

Bitterness comes to us after we have been treated unjustly, or after circumstances have destroyed something in our lives, and we choose to meditate upon that, instead of upon God, and His goodness to us. We are instructed in Philippians 4:8 to think about things that are good, pure, and just. God gives us the ability to allow Him to deal with the problems we face, while we simply trust in Him, if we will meditate upon His goodness, instead of the wrongs in the world.

Wrath, anger, and clamour go hand in hand with bitterness. If we choose to focus on the wrongs done to us, our minds will be filled with thoughts of making things right in our perspective, instead of letting God deal with things. Once someone allows themselves to get to this point, evil speaking is next in line, and there is no possible way for us to live pure and clean lives with these things at the forefront of our minds. God knows that if we go down this road, we will only add to the problems in our lives, and Satan knows that if he can get us to think this way, he can quickly ruin our lives, and our families, with the very sins that God has already given us victory over.

Because of this seed of gentleness that has been planted by the Holy Spirit, we have the ability to be kind, even to those who are unkind to us. This fruit makes us capable of being tenderhearted, even to those who abuse us. Because of the fruit, God has make it possible for us to forgive those who have done us wrong, even when they do not deserve it. We have the example of Jesus Christ, throughout His life, and even as He was upon the Cross, His goal was the forgiveness of those who had done Him wrong.

God does not command us to be gentle beings because He takes pleasure in seeing us struggle. He has given us this command because His goal is to make us better, stronger Christians. He has given us this command because He knows the power that bitterness has upon our lives, and how quickly bitterness can turn into hatred, and how hatred can destroy our lives. This fruit is designed to set us apart in this world, giving those who are lost a chance to see His changing power in our lives.

Finally, this fruit can be used to stop situations from escalating when we are dealing with conflict. We read in Proverbs 15:1, "A soft answer turneth away wrath, but grievous words stir up anger." God didn't give us salvation so that we can continue living like the rest of the world; He gave it so that we have the wonderful gift of eternal life, and so the world might see Him, through us. We have the choice of being the people He wants us to be, or ignoring His direction, continuing to act like we are our own master. Each one of us will face opposition from the world, and how we deal with it will determine the eternal outcome for many of the people we have contact with daily.

This fruit of gentleness is available to us every day. By keeping our hearts fertile for it to produce, we will have the benefit of the filth of the world not being able to contaminate us, drawing us back into a life of sin and bondage. It will also allow God to use us to make a huge impact upon the world around us. Will you allow this Godly fruit to grow in your life today?

FRUITS OF THE SPIRIT: GOODNESS

Galatians 5:22-23, "But the fruit of the Spirit is love, joy, peace, longsuffering, gentleness, goodness, faith, meekness, temperance: against such there is no law."

Everyone knows at least one person that they would call a "good" person. This person is the kind of person who makes an impact upon the world of everyone they come into contact with. People who have had dealings with this person will remember him or her for many years to come, and maybe for a lifetime. When we look at our lives, each one of us want to be known as this kind of person. What many do not know, is how to be this person.

The definition of a good person is someone who conforms his or her life and conversation to behave benevolently toward others. Think of that person who has made such an impact upon your life. What was it about them that spoke so deeply into your soul? It was the fact that they were willing to do without things they wanted or needed, in order to provide for the needs of those they came in contact with. They studied the people around them, and knew the needs they had, and they were willing to do whatever it took to provide that need.

In a world in which selfishness has become so prevalent, this trait is almost unheard of. Many people are willing to sacrifice any amount of people to achieve their own goals, sparing no expense to their fellow man, if it takes them one step closer to where they want to be. Along with this, they have love for no one but themselves, and have zero compassion for anyone, even family members.

The Apostle Paul had this to say in Romans 7:18, "For I know that in me (that is, in my flesh,) dwelleth no good thing: for to will is present with me; but how to perform that which is good I find not." We each struggle with selfish desires in life. We each find ourselves putting ourselves, and our dreams, before others. Paul was no different. He admits here to wanting to be this good person, but finding himself unable to do it. He talks about the good that he wants to do, he ends up not doing, but the evil things he hates, and doesn't want to do are the things he ends up doing.

The very same can be said for each one of us. We try to fight the desires we have for sinful things in our own power, and every time, we find ourselves unable to do what we know we need to do. The reason we keep going back to the same sins over and over again is that we have a sin nature. This sin nature overpowers the good that we want to do, causing us to be everything except for the good person we want to be.

The only way to overcome this problem we have is to submit to the Holy Spirit, giving Him power in our lives, letting Him have full control of us, giving up our desires and replacing them with His desires, no matter the cost to us. As we learn to do this, we will find that good begins to take the place of bad in our lives. Yes, we will still struggle with sins, because our sin nature still remains present with us until death. But the longer we submit to God, the less we will struggle with sin in our lives.

As you look back on your life, you probably have many regrets, as do I. There were times that we strayed from the path the Lord has given us, wanting to go our own way, and do our own thing. These are the times of deep regret for us, and the times in life that have done the most damage to us, and those we love. While at the time it seemed that we were enjoying ourselves, we can now look back to see these are the times that have torn down and destroyed the good we might have done.

If we are willing to let the Holy Spirit grow this fruit of goodness in our lives, we will have many fewer of these times to be ashamed of when we look back at the end of our lives. If we will submit to God, we can be people who are remembered for good, instead of destruction. If we will allow God to build what He wants to build in our lives, our children and grandchildren will be able, one day, to think of us, and the huge impact we made in their lives for the Lord.

FRUITS OF THE SPIRIT: FAITH

Galatians 5:22-23, "But the fruit of the Spirit is love, joy, peace, longsuffering, gentleness, goodness, faith, meekness, temperance: against such there is no law."

The meaning of the seventh Fruit of the Spirit, faith, is a personal measurement of the level of confidence in what Christ has done and will do in, through, and for us. It is absolutely imperative that we have, and are steadily growing, our faith. No matter where you are at in life, and no matter how long you have been a Christian, the fact is that if your faith is not growing stronger, it is growing weaker. The Bible tells us in Romans 12:3 that God has given every person a measure of faith. Every person who has ever lived has been given faith. We use it as we turn the key in the ignition of our vehicles, as we flip the light switch, and when we turn on the water faucet. Faith is a part of every day life, but also a huge and vital part of the Christian's walk in this world. We choose, every day, what we will put our faith into, and if we will do what is necessary to strengthen it; but the question is, how can we strengthen it.

Faith is what gives us the strength to keep serving God when it looks as though we will lose everything. Faith is what helps us to remain focused on the Lord when the chances for worldly success come our way, but it would cost us our relationship with Jesus Christ. Faith is what keeps us from going to the places our flesh wants to go; those places where our favorite sins can be easily found. Ephesians 2:8 tells us, "For by grace are ye saved, through faith, and that not of yourselves; it is the gift of God." Hebrews 11:6 says, "But without faith it is impossible to please God." Friend, faith is not only the doorway to salvation, but it is the only we will ever find to please God.

As with every other Fruit of the Spirit, we can either give this fruit good ground, to make it grow, or we can uproot it in our hearts, making it weak and unable to make a difference in our lives. The path that leads to a strong faith is hard, but well worth the sacrifices we will make to achieve it. As we look again at the meaning of faith, we see that our level of faith depends upon our level of confidence in the Lord. As we depend on, and trust Him, in the small things, we will see how He has taken care of our needs, and even many of our desires. After we see His provision in these little things, our confidence in His faithfulness gets stronger. As we learn to trust Him more fully, He will bring us to larger and larger battles, and this is what creates a strong faith in us. We learn to trust Him when we learn that we must depend upon Him. We learn to trust Him more and more as we are able to think back to the many times He has seen us through difficult times.

To be successful in this faith walk, we must come to the point that we realize we are completely dependent upon Him, in every aspect of life. It is easy to believe and follow Him when things are all going our way; but when the path gets steep and rocky, we often find ourselves trying to find an easier way to go. We leave the path that He has put us on, determined to walk in our own strength. It is in these times, especially, that we must keep our eyes on the goal, and keep following God.

Romans 10:17, "Faith cometh by hearing, and hearing by the Word of God." Not only is our faith developed, or hindered, by the way we follow God, it is greatly affected by the amount of time that we spend hearing the Word of God. Hearing is not just letting the words fall upon deaf ears, but listening to, and meditating upon, Scripture. We should make it a priority to be in a church where the true Word of God is taught, and we should make it a part of our daily life outside of Church as well. The more we know of the Word, the more we will have a chance to abide by what it says. Friend, the Lord is ready, willing, and able to help you in your life, no matter what you need help with. He wants you to have a faith that can move the mountains in your life, but ultimately, the choice is yours; His desire for you will not overpower your freedom to choose what you will do with the faith He has given you.

FRUITS OF THE SPIRIT: MEEKNESS

Galatians 5:22-23, "But the fruit of the Spirit is love, joy, peace, longsuffering, gentleness, goodness, faith, meekness, temperance: against such there is no law."

If one looks up the definition of meekness in the dictionary today, he would see two definitions: "1) humbly patient or docile, as under provocation from others; 2) overly submissive or compliant; spiritless; tame." If we look at the life of Jesus Christ, and the examples He has given us, we quickly begin to understand that neither of these definitions are an accurate description of the life of Jesus Christ, nor are they what He has commanded us to be and do.

Because the English language has changed, it is always better to go back to a dictionary that was in use at the time of the printing of the King James Bible. The 1828 Webster gives us the Bible's true meaning of the word meekness; **Softness of temper; mildness; gentleness; forbearance under injuries and provocations.**

The eighth fruit of the Spirit is meekness, and it is one we would all do well to have an abundance of in our lives. It goes against everything that comes naturally in us to be meek mannered people. When someone miss treats us or lies to us, our natural response is to put them in their place, and let others know about how we were treated by this person. But the response God wants us to give is a response of meekness, combined with the previous seven fruits we have talked about. While it may go against everything we would like to do, the spiritual benefits it gives us is astounding. The person who lives in a spirit of meekness may be trampled upon by the world, but in letting this fruit have its way in our lives, we will have lives that will be remembered: lives that will have eternal impact on those we come into contact with.

The person who allows this fruit to grow in their lives will have a softness of temper unlike anything they could do by themselves. The meekness of Jesus Christ allowed Him, as a perfect man, to walk with men who were full of struggles and problems, teaching them how to lead others to a God they could never have known otherwise. Because He was mild mannered, He repeatedly showed love and compassion to those who hated Him, and wanted Him dead. Though they tried to kill Him, He was able to reach out to them with the love of a God who wanted to have a relationship with them.

Jesus was also a gentle person because of His meekness. He alone had the power, and the right, to refuse to forgive the sins of mankind. He forgave men, not because He was forced to, but because He chose to. As He hung upon an unjust Cross, condemned by unjust men for crimes He never would have even thought of committing, He had legions of angles waiting for His call to come and take Him down. Because He allowed meekness to personify who He was, He chose to take the punishment that you and I should have rightfully faced.

As we think of this wonderful fruit of meekness, and how it would impact not only our lives, but every life we come into contact with, we would do well to remember the meekness of our Lord and Savior, as He hung upon a Cross and took our sins upon Himself. This precious fruit has been planted in the heart of every believer, and just waits to be nourished into something that will change our outlook on life, and make us the Christians that we are commanded to be.

We each have a choice today. Will we go out with meekness, showing a world that is lost and undone the love of a Savior, and showing them that the love of this Savior makes changes that cannot be make believe? Will we chose to endure the unjust hardships of the world to insure that the unbelievers in our lives have a chance to see Him? Or will we continue to suppress this life changing fruit, showing the world around us that Christ hasn't really made a difference in our hearts?

FRUITS OF THE SPIRIT: TEMPERANCE

Galatians 5:22-23, "But the fruit of the Spirit is love, joy, peace, longsuffering, gentleness, goodness, faith, meekness, temperance: against such there is no law."

The final Fruit of the Spirit we see in this passage is the fruit of temperance. Webster's tells us that temperance is "the practice of always controlling your actions, thoughts, or feelings so that you do not eat or drink too much, become too angry, etc."

We can all testify to the fact that we do not always meet the definition of temperance. When sandpaper people or situations come into our lives and stay too long, we can easily lose anything that can resemble self-control. Even when we start out with the best of intentions, we sometimes find that we can very quickly get out of control.

This is true of our attitudes, actions and choices. We can probably all think of many times in our own lives when we decided to "turn over a new leaf," or find the problem shortly after our many "New Year's Resolutions." Paul tells us in the seventh chapter of Romans that he found that he consistently does the things that he hates to do, and consistently fails to do the things that he wants to do. He tells us the reason is because there are two people inside us, fighting for the supreme rule over our bodies. Friend, we can truly love the Lord Jesus Christ, while at the same time fighting over and over again the very same battles with sin and stronghold that we have fought our whole lives. The only answer that will bring true and lasting results in your strongholds, and mine, is the answer of allowing the Spirit to produce this fruit of temperance in our lives.

It is only the Holy Spirit that can give us control when we are surrounded by enemies on all sides. It is only the Holy Spirit that can allow us to change our decision making process when it comes to sins that we have held on to for so many years. Sure, we can do it for a while on our own, but sooner or later, we will fall back into our old ways. The Spirit has the power to pull our thoughts back when we would allow them to get away from us. He is able to help us change, but we must be willing to allow Him the power in our lives to make the changes He wants to make.

The path to real change is a very hard path, and it is impossible to either find, or to stay on, in our own power. This is why He has given the fruit of temperance to us. To make full use of this fruit, the Christian must be willing to stay focused upon Christ completely. This willingness must be accompanied by the willingness to remove ourselves from people, places, and things that will make us go contrary to the will of God in our lives. It will mean getting rid of some friends that want to steer us wrong. It will mean a change in our reading and viewing habits.

Friend, do you find yourself wanting and needing to make changes in your life, without seeing any lasting change coming? Do you find yourself losing control in situations where you cannot afford to lose control? Why not give the power you cannot find in your life to make changes that are desperately needed over to the God who is fully capable of keeping you in control?

"But the fruit of the Spirit is love, joy, peace, longsuffering, gentleness, goodness, faith, meekness, temperance: against such there is no law." These fruits that have been given to the Christian are able to completely change our outlook on life. They give us the ability to live our lives as Christ has commanded us to live. They want to take root in your life and mine. They want to make us look more like Christ. They want to use our lives to be a light that draws others who are lost in sin and addiction to the One who can make the only change that has eternal impact. Will you allow them to grow and become healthy in your life?

WINNING THOSE YOU DON'T UNDERSTAND

1 Corinthians 9:19-22, "For though I be free from all men, yet have I made myself servant unto all, that I might gain the more. And unto the Jews I became a Jew, that I might gain the Jews; to them that are under the law, as under the law, that I might gain them that are under the law; To them that are without law, as without law, (being not without law to God, but under the law to Christ,) that I might gain them that are without law. To the weak became I as weak, that I might gain the weak: I am made all things to all men, that I might by all means save some."

As a Christian, the Bible makes it very clear that you are to be different; a peculiar person, relying upon God and God alone for your needs. A Christian who understands this, and lives it, is in the truest form "free from all men." But many Christians take this idea to mean that they owe no person anything at all, even common courtesy, or worse yet, being a witness to the lost and dying world around them.

Paul is building up here to what most of us know as the "great love chapter" of the Bible. Because of the love and concern he had for the people of the world, he was willing to do whatever it took to win them to Christ. In Romans 9:1-3 we can read about the continual burden he had for his fellow man; a burden that was so great that he declares he would be willing to be accursed from Christ for them to know Christ. What great love he had for men!

Some of the fruit from this love is that he took great care to study, know, and understand the people he was sent as a witness to. His was the attitude that, though he was free from all men and didn't need to worry about what they thought of him, his love for them compelled him to make himself a servant to them. Instead of just coming to them preaching about the judgment and wrath of God, he also preached about the love and mercy of God. Instead of just coming to preach and teach to them, he came looking for ways that he could be of service to them in some way.

Paul knew that the key to the heart is not just in knowing the Word of God, but in showing the love of God through his willingness to understand the lifestyle and hardships of those he ministered to. No matter what the task was, Paul was there to help. No matter where the community was, when Paul came to witness to it, he became a part of it.

Is there someone in your life that has done this for you? Chances are, your answer is yes, at least to some point. It is when you saw the love and compassion for Christ that you began to want to know more about Him. It is when you saw the faithfulness of Christ that you began to want a personal relationship with Him. You didn't see these things from Christ Himself, you saw them in the life of the one who introduced you to your Savior.

Is there someone in your life that you would love to see begin that personal relationship with the Lord? Is there a group somewhere in your community that is not being reached for Christ for some reason? Maybe you and I should start asking ourselves these questions. Have we taken the time to truly know the people that we just can't seem to reach for Christ? Do we understand what makes them like they are; what makes them act the way they act?

Until we begin to approach people with this same attitude Paul had, we will never be effective for Christ. In fact, we are probably turning more people away from Him because of our lack of love and compassion for them. It is only after we become accepted by the people we are trying to reach that we will ever begin to reach them. And at this point, we will be able to say, as Paul said, "I am made all things to all men, that I might by all means save some."

RUNNING THE RACE

1 Corinthians 9:24-27, "Know ye not that they which run in a race run all, but one receiveth the prize? So run, that ye may obtain. And every man that striveth for the mastery is temperate in all things. Now they do it to obtain a corruptible crown; but we an incorruptible. I therefore so run, not as uncertainly; so fight I, not as one that beateth the air. But I keep under my body, and bring it into subjection: lest that by any means, when I have preached to others, I myself should be a castaway."

Paul talked much about running races, and what was required of one to run a race, and be competitive in it. We can be assured that he was not talking about running a physical race in these passages. He used language that everyone would understand in that day. Let's look at what is required of us to run the race of our life.

There are many different types of races we can find ourselves in, but the most important race of all is the spiritual one. Each person alive today in this world is running a spiritual race, though many do not know it. We all run together; we are all born into this world. But as we look at the world around us, it is plain to see that we are not all going the same direction or the same speed. Some get caught up in the muck and mire of wrong decisions. Some will get lost at major cross roads in life. Many will stumble and fall because of wrong teaching. The list goes on and on. Everyone who runs will not win!

For us to win this race there is much training and discipline required. We all want to win! It is a drive that runs deep in the heart of every person. Paul gives us several items of absolute necessity in order to "receive the prize." First is temperance. The picture here is someone that is self-restrained. Many people have no understanding of this at all. We live in America, and we want what we want, when we want it, and there is no excuse for having any less at any time in our lives. This is why most Americans are head over heels in debt! We must learn to be moderate, or self-restrained. Paul goes on to say that people running the races of life are running for a corruptible crown—in our case it may be money, or popularity, or status, or the best looking significant other. But all these things will get old, worn out, and dusty. Very soon, they will mean nothing at all! Paul says we should be running for a crown that will never lose its luster! This is running in a spiritual way.

Secondly, we should run and fight with certainty. We should know where we are, and who our battle is with, at all times. Never lose sight of the fact that Satan is going to throw everything at us that he can throw. He knows our weaknesses, and he will certainly use them against us. The only way we can run and fight with certainty is to run as close to Jesus Christ as possible. Keep godly friends, who will hold us accountable when we do wrong; ones who will call us and ask us where we were when we missed church yesterday.

And last, but not least, we must keep our bodies under subjection. In many cases, this may prove to be the hardest thing do here. Our bodies want to tell us when to sleep, when to drink, when to eat, and even what to eat and drink. Many people let their bodies rule over almost every aspect in their lives. It is hard to fight our body. It is easier to eat and drink to satisfy our cravings than to get off the couch and do the exercises we need to do to be healthy. It is so very easy to give in to the desires our bodies have because of the bad decisions we have made in the past. But if we do not rule the body, we will serve the body!

Paul is talking about running a race, with the intention of winning! No one runs with the intention of coming in second or third. God offers us the help we need to become winners in our personal race. Isn't it about time we give up a race we cannot win, and give it over to a God who cannot lose?

FORMULA FOR FAILURE

1 Corinthians 10:11-12, "Now all these things happened unto them for ensamples; and they are written for our admonition, upon whom the ends of the world are come. Wherefore let him that thinketh he standeth take heed lest he fall."

History is filled with people who have grown to greatness from obscurity. The stories of these great people are told over and over throughout our schools, families, workplaces, and churches. These men and women are highly honored and respected by anyone who has goals for great achievement in life. Their lives and actions are studied very thoroughly so that the person aspiring for greatness can learn how to better reach their goals in life.

We can also all think of some people in our lifetimes who have fallen from greatness to nothingness. These people, while just as famous as those who have found and kept success, are ones that are shunned and forgotten by most of us. We don't care to think about them because they are a reminder of how quickly success can become utter failure.

Scripture tells of many great men that ruined their lives, their families, and who cost their countries in devastating ways. God doesn't have their stories in the Bible so that we can feel sorry for, or make fun of the failures we see; they are in the Word of God so that you and I may see their mistakes, and learn from them, so that we do not make the same terrible decisions that were made by them.

Chapter ten of 1 Corinthians begins by letting the reader understand that these men were the same kind of men as everyone else. They were not picked out by God for failure, for the purpose of being used as examples. These men had the same chances that everyone else around them had. They had lived their lives, not above the people, but with the people. They had heard and seen the same promises and warnings from God that you and I can hear today. They had all seen the power and protection of God on many occasions. It should also be noted that they lived with the same temptations that you and I live with today. They were, simply, people like us. They wanted what was best for their families. But they somehow got sidetracked, or ambushed, by their enemy. Their stories are in Scripture so that we might take warning of how quickly sin can overwhelm even the best of us.

Verse seven begins a list of warnings to the believer. It warns of things that begin very small in life, but, if given place in our hearts, can and will grow very quickly to the destruction of our Christian walk. It tells us first to not be idolaters. An idol is anything that we esteem more important than the Lord. It can be anything from a job, a vehicle, a spouse, or other family member. The Lord demands that the Christian put Him first in our lives. He wants to be the absolute most important thing to us. God has given us many wonderful things in life, but the day we begin to let any of these wonderful things become more important to us than He is, is the day we begin our fall.

Secondly, the Christian is warned against fornication. The meaning of this word is to have sex before marriage. Society today overlooks this as a sin, and sadly, so does many churches. It is so commonplace today that it is simply accepted by a great majority of people. But God's Word never changes, nor does His expectations for His people. He created sex to be a beautiful thing between a man and a woman, after marriage. We have grown up in a world that sees nothing wrong with this behavior, but God says it is a great wrong. 1 Corinthians 6:18 tells us that every other sin is without the body, but this sin is against our bodies. Friend, if we want to be able to stand in the blessings of God, we must change our attitudes and convictions to match God's. He takes it very seriously when we ignore His plan!

Next we are told not to tempt Christ. Though God is a patient and loving God, we place ourselves in great danger when we try His patience, or do things to provoke His anger. Many Christians live in known sin, refusing to take action to remove it from their lives, simply because they believe God will allow them to get away what they are doing. Because they see that God has proven Himself to be longsuffering and patient, they believe they have plenty of time to take care of things later. 1 Thessalonians 5:19 warns us not to quench the Spirit. We cannot continue to believe the lie that God will let His people continue to live in sin without consequence! When He reveals an area of sin in our lives, He means for us to take care of it immediately. If we choose not to, we may not be given another chance.

Finally, we are told to not murmur against the Lord. Probably daily, we have many chances to murmur our complaints to Him, to feel sorry for ourselves for the things He has allowed to come into our lives. Once we give in to the desire to complain, the enemy will make sure that our eyes are very open to anything we can possibly complain about. These complaints will quickly overshadow, and overcome, the things we have to be grateful and thankful for. They will suck any joy and faith we have right out of our lives. They will make us forget that God loves us; they will make us forget that Jesus gave His life for us.

God has given us these warnings because He loves us beyond measure. He knows well how quickly our lives can be destroyed. He knows very well the power that Satan has to make us see the bad in every situation, and He knows that Satan's desire is to make sure we live our Christian life in failure. The Lord also knows that we are most in danger of allowing these deadly influences into our lives after a period of success or victory in some area. "Wherefore let him that thinketh he standeth take heed lest he fall."

VICTORY, EVEN OVER DEATH!

1 Corinthians 15:54-58, "So when this corruptible shall have put on incorruption, and this mortal shall have put on immortality, then shall be brought to pass the saying that is written, death is swallowed up in victory. O death, where is thy sting? O grave, where is thy victory? The sting of death is sin; and the strength of sin is the law. But thanks be to God, which giveth us the victory through our Lord Jesus Christ. Therefore, my beloved brethren, be ye steadfast, unmovable, always abounding in the work of the Lord, forasmuch as ye know that your labour is not in vain in the Lord."

It is very easy for the Christian to become discouraged in this world. It is even easier for the one who is trying to overcome deep seated sin to become discouraged. This world is set up against the Christian, and against anyone who would try to live a life of good morals, and good works. The people of the world love darkness, and hate for any form of a light to be shined upon their dark lives, and they will fight against anyone who tries to display a life that uplifts Jesus Christ.

In these times of discouragement, God wants us to remember that we are not fighting for this world, or the things that can be found in this world. Everything we see is what the Scriptures call corruptible; it will not last any longer than this world. If we work toward earthly riches, and earthly recognition, the reward we receive will only last as long as our life here on this earth. But the Christian has so much more to look forward to, and to live for! These verses are given to give encouragement to the Christian when he faces the hatefulness of the world around him.

The lost person will lose everything at the time of death, even if they hold great riches. They can take nothing with them. This is the sting of death, and the final victory of the grave. This is something the Christian will never have to fear. As we work for the Lord upon this earth, we earn riches that will be taken into the next life. If you look around you, and see nothing worth living for, you can be sure that the enemy has been working, and has gotten you to take your focus off of the things that truly matter.

The last two verses of our passage should be enough to make even the weakest Christian jump for joy. Even in times of struggle and failure in this life, we can know for certain that we have been granted the victory in the things that matter the most. God has given you the victory in battles that you don't even know about yet! God has granted you victory in the struggles you are having right now, if you are willing to trust and follow Him, no matter what. Victory over the stronghold that have accumulated in your spiritual and personal life is yours, bought and paid for by Jesus Christ! He offers this victory, free of charge, if only you will put your faith in Him, following Him with your whole heart.

Because of the victory He has already won, the Christian has the power to be steadfast and unmovable in this life. We have an endless source of power to overcome temptation and adversity in this life, through faith in Jesus Christ. Because of Christ, we can live full and fruitful lives in the midst of the desert of life. We can have joy, and much success in the work that the Lord has given us to do, even while facing the hatred and ridicule of the world in which we live. God has promised to give us grace enough to see us through the times in life that would be unbearable in our own power. God has promised us mercy when we stumble and fall, and an uplifting hand to get us back on the path He has put before us. God has promised to light our path with His Word, and He has promised that the load we will bear will be lighter, and easier, than the burden those without faith have to bear alone.

If all this isn't enough, we can also know that the things we do for Him will never be done in vain. He is keeping a record of the things we do. He is keeping a record of our faithfulness in times of hardship and distress, and anything that we might lose in this life for Him, will be regained in the life to come. There is no other god who can make these kinds of promises!

Do you find yourself discouraged in this life? Have you been ready to throw in the towel, thinking that this life of faith is not what you thought it would be? If so, think of the promises He has given, and remember that He tells us that this world is not our home. He does not tell you to work for the things of this world, but the things of the next world. Put your eyes upon Him, and let Him give you the strength to overcome this life, and to do the work He has put you here to do.

STANDING ALONE

1 Corinthians 16:13, "Watch ye, stand fast in the faith, quit you like men, be strong."

This little verse says more to the Christian than most books that are written today on any subject. Peer pressure is a way of life in all walks today, just as it has been since man was created upon the earth. The fear in our minds of what people think of us is so powerful it can often make us do things we wouldn't normally do; things we are not comfortable with doing; things we hate to do. It was present in the Garden of Eden on that day so long ago when mankind made the fatal leap into sin, casting himself upon his own understanding, and casting God's loving warnings into the trash. It is often present when the Church starts down the slippery slope of compromise. It is present when many teenagers take their first drink or ingest their first drug. It is present many times when the adult makes that decision to commit a crime or walk away from their family. And it will be present when each one of us is dead and gone on to eternity.

We will never outgrow the effects of peer pressure. To the contrary, its power and effects on us seem to actually get stronger as we get older. Maybe we have been faced with failure several times in life, and the ever-present enemy is there, whispering in our ear that we just need to give up or give in, and do what the rest of the world is doing. Maybe we see our friends and former classmates way up on the "ladder of success," while we are barely hanging on and losing our grip. Whatever the reason, we find, as we pay close attention to our lives, many of the things we do are a result of peer pressure. We want to find a place to belong. We want to fit in with those we are around.

What Paul is telling the Corinthians, and us, is that we should defy the power of peer pressure, no matter what the world says. We know what God wants for us; we know the power He has to change the situation, no matter how bad it seems. God wants us to stand firm on our beliefs. He wants us to rely on Him for whatever that need or desire is that is so prominent in our lives. Don't take the world's short cuts in life, thinking they will get you where you want to be sooner or more efficiently than God's plan can get you there.

By taking this stand, you will be sure to be made fun of by friends and family. You will also probably lose some of the Christian friends you have; but those friends have already been blinded by their plans and desires, and cannot see clearly. If you know something is wrong, there is only one choice, no matter what the cost might be; get away from it! Don't be held up by what others think and allow your life to be ruined. Trust God when He promises in Romans 8:28 that He will make all things work together for good to those who love Him. Take the stand that needs to be taken!

Paul tells us here to watch; to wait with expectation for something. Stand firm on your Biblical beliefs and wait for God to come through, even if everyone walks away from you. Have the attitude that it only matters what God thinks of you! Live your life to please Him, and honor and glorify Him, no matter if it cost you every friend you have. At the end of the race, it will not matter even a little bit how many people thought you were crazy.

Paul tells us to be strong. Even when we know we are weak, we can be strong in the faith, if we put God's desires above our own. Peer pressure also works both ways. If your Christian brothers and sisters see you taking the stand that needs to be taken, it will give them the strength to stand with you. It may be that God has put you in the situation you find yourself in because He knows that with the stand you will take today, others will find the power to do the same.

TRUE CONFESSION

1 John 1:9, "If we confess our sins, He is faithful and just to forgive us our sins, and to cleanse us from all unrighteousness."

One of the hardest things to understand in the Christian life is the aspect of forgiveness that God freely gives us. We have done so many things to hurt and destroy every good thing He has given us in life, yet He still offers, with no strings attached, His forgiveness. It is ours for the taking, if we will but confess our sins to Him. This idea is on such a high level that we simply cannot grasp it. The best we can do is to just read it, accept it, and embrace it with thankfulness to our Heavenly Father.

Our verse says our part is to simply confess our sins. But we need to fully understand what this means. Many have the idea that confession is simply to state that we did something. While this is certainly a part of confession, it is only the beginning of the path we must take if we want to get the full benefit of this verse. Our watered down version of confession today can be likened to getting a toddler to admit that he stole cookies from the cookie jar while our back was turned to him. He will argue, blame, give excuses, and flat out lie about taking them, even while the crumbs of evidence are all around his feet on the floor. We can get a confession out of him, even while he tries to shift the focus somewhere else.

To confess, in God's eyes means, "to agree" to something; to "own it." God knows we sinned, we know we sinned, and the whole world around us knows we sinned. God is not looking for the back handed confession of a two year old; He wants us to put the blame where it belongs: ON OURSELF. God wants our attitude while coming to Him to be one of not only knowing we have failed, but understanding and agreeing with Him that our failure can only be blamed on one person. He has given us every opportunity and tool to do right, and we turned our back on right to do wrong. This is true confession. Another part of confession that we do not like to think very hard about is the attitude that we will try to abstain from this particular sin in the future. God knows our heart when we come to ask His forgiveness to only clear our conscious until tomorrow when we have every intention of doing the very same thing over. Repentance is very much a part of true confession. Friend, if you are confessing your sins while at the same time making plans of returning to them, you may as well just save your breath; God will not honor this confession.

Once we understand what true confession is, and decide to take action on it, we can expect several things from our Heavenly Father. First, we see that He is faithful. The definition of this word is simple, but so profound: "Constant; not fickle; as a faithful lover or friend." This verse promises us that our Father is constant. He is the one constant in an ever changing universe. We can absolutely depend on His Word to remain true no matter what changes in life. When Scripture tells us He is faithful, it means every time we confess, no matter what, how much, or what the damage was.

Next, we see that He is just. The meaning here is; "conformed to rules of justice; doing equal justice." Scripture tells us in Romans 2:11 that God is not a respecter of persons. While we may look at wealthy people or people in power as better than us, God sees no difference; we are all His creation, we have all sinned, and we each need His forgiveness the same. God will do equal justice to every person; past, present, and future, who truly confesses to Him. He requires no more or no less from anyone than that they confess.

Next, we can expect God to "forgive us our sins." The meaning of this word is "to pardon; to remit, as an offense or debt; to overlook an offense, and treat the offender as not guilty." Can you imagine? We, who have spent a lifetime destroying, ignoring, and turning away from His love, can be looked at by a perfectly sinless and righteous God as though we have never sinned! Before our true confession, God could only see our unrighteousness. After confession, God can only see the righteousness of Jesus Christ, His Son!

Finally, we see that He will "cleanse us from all unrighteousness." He not only forgives our sins; He will clean us up! The picture here is clearly that He will forgive us (make us as if we have not sinned), but will go on to clean up that sinful lifestyle and get us to the point that we no longer do that sin. Don't misunderstand; I am not saying that we will ever live a sinless life. We are imperfect humans. But He will not leave us to wander around in our darkness; He will clean up our life.

Once we start living a life of true confession, we will quickly begin to have less and less desire to do the sins we once enjoyed! Each day we live this verse, God is able to clean us up a little more. We should be able to look back on past years of our life as see a huge difference between that day and this. Many Christians choose to live a life of defeat because they never come to Him with true confession.

I challenge you to examine your life today. How do you approach this verse? Do you confess to God like the two year old, coming only because you have to, or are you reaching out to Him, crying, "Abba, Father, I have sinned, the blame is mine, and I can do nothing about it!" If you will come to Him seeking not just a clear conscious, but a clean heart and life, His promise to you is lined with the gold of His hand of mercy and grace in your life.

FORGIVENESS AND CLEANSING

1 John 1:9, "If we confess our sins, He is faithful and just to forgive us our sins, and to cleanse us from all unrighteousness."

God gives us such a wonderful promise in this verse. He promises to forgive us of our sins, if only we will confess them to Him. He promises this forgiveness for any and every sin we commit. There is no exception, and there is no sin too great or small for Him to forgive us of. But the condition of receiving this forgiveness is our confession.

To confess means to "agree" with something. Many people go through life making excuses for the sins they commit. Each one of us has a choice to make about how we will approach this verse. Every person who sins can find an excuse to give about the reason we have sinned. Many use their loved ones for this excuse, saying that they did something to them, and caused a similar action to be taken in retribution. Some use their childhood, saying that their parents mistreated them, or that they didn't have parents. But the fact is that we each have the freedom to make decisions about which action to take, or which words come out of our mouths. Even if someone mistreats us, we make the choice to either honor, or dishonor God with our lives. When we choose to dishonor Him, we choose to sin. God offers forgiveness, even when we knowingly dishonor Him, with the condition that we confess our sins as our actions and decisions, instead of trying to place blame upon another party. He wants us to agree with Him, that it was a wrong choice, and brought dishonor to Him.

We must also consider the last phrase in this verse: "and to cleanse us from all unrighteousness." When we approach God, confessing and asking for His forgiveness, we must approach Him with a desire to change. God is not in the business of forgiving us so that we can go right back out five minutes later, already determined to commit the same sin again. If we approach Him with this attitude, we are not truly confessing our sins, but only trying to ease our conscience. God knows the condition of our hearts, even before we come to Him, and He will not waste His time with someone who simply wants to play the religion game. Galatians 6:7 tells us, "Be not deceived; God is not mocked: for whatsoever a man soweth, that shall he also reap." God offers complete forgiveness to us for our sins, but we must ask for this forgiveness with the right attitude, and the right attitude is to approach Him for forgiveness, and cleansing.

As we approach Him with these things in mind, and with a true desire for healing and cleansing, He forgives us, and cleanses us, of our sins. This is not to say that we will never commit these same sins again, because we may slip back into the same pit we are trying to get out of. But if we will truly confess, ask forgiveness, and seek the cleansing that only He can provide, we will see a change in our hearts, and this will overflow into our actions and attitudes.

When we come to Him with the attitude of 1 John 1:9, we will quickly find that the times we allow ourselves to go back to the same sin, we experience a godly sorrow for committing these sins. We begin to understand that our relationship is broken with our loving Father because we willingly do things that hurt Him. This is the wonderful thing about being not only forgiven, but cleansed, from our sins! If we received forgiveness without cleansing, He would expect us to remain in a life of sin. But because of the cleansing He gives, we are restored into a beautiful relationship with Him, and when we allow sin back in, we find that it not only hurts Him, but us as well.

Have you found yourself coming to God, asking forgiveness simply to ease your conscience for living a life that you know is fake Christianity? Have you asked for His forgiveness while making plans to continue the very thing you are coming to Him about? If you and I really want freedom and contentment in this life, the only way to achieve it is by asking not only for forgiveness of these sins, but by allowing Him to cleanse us from these very sins, and removing them from our hearts.

A FRIEND IN GOD

1 Samuel 28:16-20, "Then said Samuel, Wherefore then dost thou ask of me, seeing the LORD is departed from thee, and is become thine enemy? And the LORD hath done to him, as He spake by me: for the LORD hath rent the kingdom out of thine hand, and given it to thy neighbor, even to David: Because thou obeyedst not the voice of the LORD, nor executedst His fierce wrath upon Amalek, therefore hath the LORD done this thing unto thee this day. Moreover the LORD will also deliver Israel with thee into the hand of the Philistines: and tomorrow shalt thou and thy sons be with me: the LORD also shall deliver the host of Israel into the hand of the Philistines. Then Saul fell straightway all along on the earth, and was sore afraid, because of the words of Samuel: and there was no strength in him: for he had eaten no bread all the day, nor all the night."

At this point in Saul's life, he had rejected the commands of God several times. God had departed from him, and would not answer any of his prayers. As Saul had always been a man that would do what he wanted to do, when he wanted to do it, it had not bothered him much in his everyday life. But as we come to this passage, we can see Saul's world start falling down around him very quickly. He is outnumbered by a mightier army than what he has, and is very scared. He had tried to pray to God, to no avail, then goes to the prophet to get guidance from God.

As Samuel tells him exactly what his end will be, and when, Saul undoubtedly went back to all the times he had rejected what God wanted from him. These were times when God has clearly been with him, and had clearly made known to him what he was to do. They were times when Saul knew the blessings of God, and the requirements of God, and knew the mind of God. God was on his side, because he was on God's side. In disobeying God's commands, for selfish and prideful reasons, he had brought upon himself the judgment of God. Samuel told him clearly here that God had become his enemy!

How quickly we can go from blessing to cursing in our fragile life! Once we start seeing victory in areas where we have struggled or even lived in defeat, it is easy to start thinking we have done the work ourselves. This is a very dangerous time, because we make ourselves important in our eyes instead of our Lord. We can easily be more concerned about what the world will think of us instead of what God thinks of us. If we truly look at ourselves, we will fully know that we are nothing without God; it is only by His grace and mercy that we are not consumed in our wickedness.

But even worse than the fact that we can make God our enemy, is the fact that in this passage we see clearly that our sin greatly affects the lives and well-being of everyone we come into contact with. Saul didn't just bring the judgment of God upon himself through his sins. He brought judgment upon his family, and upon his country, with great numbers of death being the outcome of one man's sin!

When we reject what God wants from us, not only do we reject His blessings, we reject His protection from our enemy! This is an enemy we can never hope to defeat. If we reject God's wishes, we open the door for Satan to defeat and destroy not only us, but those we love and care for! 1 Peter 5:8 tells us, "Be sober, be vigilant; because your adversary the devil, as a roaring lion, walketh about, seeking whom he may devour."

It is God, and God alone, who is able to keep this from happening! Let us be sober and vigilant in our lives! If we want to keep God as a friend to us, it will be done by trusting, obeying, worshipping, serving, walking with and learning from Him. With God as our friend, it will never matter how many enemies we have, for God will protect us. When the storms of life are raging, He will be our shelter. In times of famine, He will provide. He wants to be your friend; will you be His?

A LIFESTYLE OF THANKFULNESS

1 Thessalonians 5:18, "In every thing give thanks: for this is the will of God in Christ Jesus concerning you."

Most of us have probably read this verse many times. We have also probably heard sermons that use this verse. But, if we are honest, most of us would have to say that we have not lived this verse in our times of hardship or conflict. It is one of those little passages of Scripture that we love to talk about, but hate to, or have no idea how to, practice in real life.

I have meditated on this verse several times in life, and had determined that what it meant was that I should remain thankful to God for His goodness and provision in even the most difficult situations I find myself in, even if I couldn't be thankful for what I am facing at the time. Indeed, the Christian should always be thankful for these things, as well as for the fact that God has promised that He will never leave us or forsake us. We should remain thankful to God every minute of every day, and seek His guidance and provision during the dark times we face.

But this verse means so very much more than that! God has opened my eyes about what He is telling us here, and about why He tells us to do something that is so impossible for us to do in our own strength. It is telling us to be thankful for everything that God brings into our lives, no matter how good or bad it may be. Don't just be thankful for the good that may come out of it; be thankful for the thing itself. I know it is much easier to say than to practice, but it is what the Lord tried to teach me for a very long time, through devastating circumstances.

Several years ago, my wife and I had been praying for the Lord to reveal His will to us, and to put us somewhere that He could use us in the ministry. He answered our prayers, and led us to a country church where we became deeply involved in. We loved it, and our family thrived there. God opened many doors in ministry there, and we gained much experience in a broad scope of ministry. He had brought us to a place where we could not only serve, but grow, as individuals and as a family.

But after being there for over two years, things began to change very quickly. One of the people in the ministry I was in decided that I was treating him wrong. We talked for a while, and I thought things had been worked out, but he refused to let it be over. The more he dwelt on the wrong that he perceived that I had done, the harder he looked for areas to place blame about. When I tried, several times, to talk to him, he refused to listen, wanting only to accuse more and more. He fabricated lies about me and about others in my family, including my children. It had become hatred within him, and he did not want to fix anything.

After many months of trying to work things out, it became clear to me that things would never be worked out with this person and me. My family and I were devastated. Because someone wanted revenge for a perceived wrong doing, it cost me the ministry I was in, it cost my family the church we were thriving in, and it cost my wife and me some friends that we have had for many years. All of this came from a man that I loved dearly; a man who I considered one of the best friends I had ever had.

Our verse says to give thanks in everything. How is it possible to thank God for something like this happening? Why would I want to be thankful for something like this? These are the questions I began asking God over and over for several months. I will never forget the day the Lord showed me the answers to my questions.

I knew I was walking very close to being bitter about this situation that had cost us so much, so I prayed that God would help me not to be bitter. I knew that my faith was being tested severely, so I prayed that God would help me to stay focused on Him and keep trusting Him. I knew that if I got on the wrong path because of this situation it would cause me to walk away from what God has called me to do, so I reminded myself daily that God has promised in Romans 8:28 to cause all things to work together for good.

I began praying that God would get me and my family through that time in our lives, but not one time did I actually thank Him for bringing us to that time. He got us through that situation, and the healing process began, but that day He really opened my eyes to the truth and depth of 1 Thessalonians 5:18.

Why should we give thanks for terrible things that happen in life? Because "this is the will of God in Christ Jesus concerning you." God wants the world to know there is a difference in living with and through Him, and just living and walking blindly through this life. He wants the unbelievers to see that He makes all the difference. And He wants you and me to know that the things that happen in our lives happen for a purpose. His purpose is to show us how much we need Him. His purpose is to make us less like the world, and more like Him. His purpose is to make us stay close to Him. His purpose is to show His glory and His love to a lost and dying world.

Several years ago I watched one of my Uncles die from a very rare form of cancer. This was a man who lived a fully devoted life for Christ. He had been in ministry for over forty years. Countless lives were forever changed because of his walk with, and his love for, the Lord. He said, just a few weeks before he died, his biggest fear was that he would dishonor God before he died. I will never forget how sweet he was, even in his pain and suffering. What an impression he made to the health care workers that took care of him.

How is it possible to give thanks for these things? It is not possible, unless we get strength from God to do it. Because my uncle lived this verse, many lives have been touched by the love of Jesus Christ that may have never known of it.

"In every thing give thanks: for this is the will of God in Christ Jesus concerning you." Nothing in life happens by chance for the Christian. God has the power to protect you, and to keep bad things from happening; he chooses to let them happen for a very specific purpose in your life. Isn't it time that God's people choose to stop fighting His will, and start embracing it for His glory and honor?

I am so thankful to God for opening my eyes to this verse. Friend, it is during the terrible times of life that God is growing His children into the people that He can use to make a true and lasting difference in the lives of others. Don't give up! Push on, and push ahead, thanking the Lord for bringing things into your life to grow you as a Christian.

A FOUNDATION WORTH BUILDING ON

2 Timothy 2:19-21, "Nevertheless the foundation of God standeth sure, having this seal, The Lord knoweth them that are His. And, Let every one that nameth the name of Christ depart from iniquity. But in a great house there are not only vessels of gold and of silver, but also of wood and of earth; and some to honor, and some to dishonor. If a man therefore purge himself from these, he shall be a vessel unto honor, sanctified, and meet for the master's use, and prepared unto every good work."

We all want to live a life that is worth remembering. Every one of us has a desire to do something great, or to be someone great, or at least to be able to look back at the end of life and know that we have accomplished something, or to have been a part of something. For many people this desire is so great in their lives that they forget the most important things. So often, we can get so devoted and focused on a goal that we find we will go to almost any means to achieve it; even if those means include going to the wrong side of the law, especially the Law of God.

It is very easy to forget that God wants us to do great things even more than we do. He created us for greatness. It is He who has put the desire in us to do, to be, and to belong. The problem comes when we let this desire be the most important thing in our lives. When this happens, we give Satan an open door into our lives. When we try to go outside of God's regulations and guidelines to accomplish something, we will find that we are fighting a battle that we cannot win.

The first thing our passage tells us is that the foundation of God stands sure. The twofold picture here is, first, that this foundation cannot be overthrown, or even harmed. The first thing a good builder does when building a house is to develop a strong foundation. I grew up in a house that did not have a foundation at all, and there was nothing in the house level or square. Every few years, Dad would have to go under the house with jacks and blocks and do his best to level the floors. A life lived without the guidelines of Scripture is just like this house. Nothing is sure; nothing is permanent.

The second picture here is that God's foundation is steady. It is not weak, nor does it change, ever. His guidelines have always been His guidelines. Though we change with time, God tells us in Malachi 3:6, "For I am the LORD; I change not..." This foundation is always in exactly the same spot. It is constant. It is a guide in place for us, that we can measure and judge ourselves. Anytime we find ourselves away from God, we can be sure that He is not the One that moved, and He cannot move to accommodate our desires; we must move to accommodate His.

The next wonderful aspect of this passage is the promise that "The Lord knoweth them that are His." It is wonderful to know that there is someone who knows us inside and out. I've been married for over twenty years, and my wife and I discover more about each other all the time. The longer we live together, the more we find out about one another. We even surprise ourselves many times, finding out something about ourselves that we didn't know. Many friendships end, or are hurt, as each person in the friendship finds out something he didn't know about his friend. But

God knows each of us better than we know ourselves, and He is still our friend even through the areas in our lives that do not line up with His standards. He will never give up on us!

These are the things that God gives us; now for our part. This is the key to living life in a great way; the door to the greatness God made us for. "Let everyone that nameth the name of Christ depart from iniquity." No matter what happens to us; no matter who wrongs us; no matter how many things go against us; God commands us to keep iniquity, or sin, out of our lives. If we know Christ as our Savior, we have this awesome foundation that God has put in place. We are a part of the greatest thing anyone will ever know. But verse twenty tells us that even in a great house there are two kinds of vessels; ones of honor, and ones of dishonor. The dishonorable ones are still part of the house. They still serve a function; they still belong in the house. But they could have been so much more than they became.

We have a choice in this life of the vessel we will be. Again, if we are truly saved, we belong in the house. The question we must now answer is; will we be everything that God knows we can be, or will we be content with just making it through the door? Verse 21 tells us that if we purge ourselves, we will be a vessel unto honor. This means if we focus on keeping sin out of our lives, God will use us to a fuller extent. The word sanctified means to be set apart for a specific use. God can use even the wicked to fulfill His will, but He asks us to be devoted enough to Him to set aside our desires and goals and make ourselves available to Him. If we will be willing to do this, He will pour down His blessings upon us, and allow us to do far greater things than we could ever accomplish on our own.

Think about how much love He has for you, and the marvelous promises He has given. He will provide the tools and materials for you to build upon the foundation He has laid. He is able to accomplish the great things through you that you could never do in your own strength. He offers you the chance to truly belong. He will give you that life worth remembering. But all of this comes only after you will lay your life's dreams and goals at His feet.

FLOATING BY FAITH

1 Timothy 1:18-19, "This charge I commit unto thee, son Timothy, according to the prophecies which went before on thee, that thou by them mightiest war a good warfare; Holding faith, and a good conscience; which some having put away concerning faith have made shipwreck:"

At the time of this writing, Timothy was a young preacher, with none of the wisdom that an old man has. We have all been young, with the world at our fingertips, and we know how exhilarating it is to step out into a brand new world. But something that comes along with a brand new world to us, are brand new ideas, brand new programs, brand new people that the enemy can use to side track us.

As we discussed in the last devotion, we each want to feel that we belong somewhere, and to do important things. It is imperative that we keep our eyes focused on the right thing, even through these desires. As we look at the world around us, we see more and more "churches" popping up everywhere. Each one has a program. Each one has a little different scheme to attract people of all ages. They are all so very different. But one thing is in common with almost all of them: They preach and teach little or no Biblical things.

Paul gives Timothy, and us, a vital lesson on living a strong Christian life that will not leave us stumbling and falling, and grabbing on to every new idea that comes around. The simple sentence he gives us is, "Holding faith, and a good conscience..."

Lack of faith is the main reason why many Christian quit. It takes a strong faith to step out into the unknown world of Christianity, especially for those coming to it from a lifestyle of addiction. Everything the Bible teaches us is contrary to what our mind tells us to do in almost every circumstance. But we must learn how to hold on to the faith, and to make our faith stronger, or the last part of our verse will certainly be our final outcome, "Which some having put away concerning faith have made shipwreck."

So how do we grow our faith? The first thing we must understand is that there is not one person alive that has more faith than the next. We can look at others and see clearly that they have done more, been more, and stepped out more than we have. We can say to ourselves that we wish we had that kind of faith. The simple truth is that we have the same amount. Romans 12: 3 says, "For I say, through the grace given unto me, to every man that is among you, not to think of himself more highly than he ought to think; but to think soberly, according as God hath dealt to every man the measure of faith." We all have the same. The secret is in that terrible word, exercise! So often young Christians get discouraged because they are not being used by God the way they want to be used. We must understand that this is just like learning a new job; it takes practice and lots of work to be effective at it!

Faith is believing in something, and if we quit when our belief is put to the test, we never really believed in it at all. James 1:3-4 tells us that the trying of our faith worketh patience, and that if we let patience have her perfect work, we will be perfect (mature), and entire, wanting nothing.

We should never get discouraged when our faith is put to the test! The enemy will try to break us, but Romans 8:28 tells us if we just trust the Lord, He will use it for our good.

Most importantly, we must never forget the source of our faith. Romans 10:17 tells us, "So then faith cometh by hearing, and hearing by the Word of God." We will never develop a strong faith if we spend no time in fellowship with God! Christian friends are good. Church is better. But the study of the Word of God is vital in our lives!

The choice is ours, and there are only two that we can make. We can choose to hold to the faith and grow strong in Christ, or we can turn away and go the same way as numerous defeated Christians, to a life of shipwreck.

GIFTED FOR THE NEXT LIFE

1 Timothy 4:14-16, "Neglect not the gift that is in thee, which was given thee by prophecy, with the laying on of the hands of the presbytery. Meditate upon these things; give thyself wholly to them; that thy profiting may appear to all. Take heed unto thyself, and unto the doctrine; continue in them: for in doing this thou shalt both save thyself, and them that hear thee."

Every Christian alive today has at least one gift that is God-given; a gift that He wants them to use for His honor and glory. Some are good at many things, but everyone is good at something. Paul is writing here to a young preacher, telling him to make sure that he does not throw away his God-given gift. Even though you may not be a preacher, and may never be, you have still been prepared for a specific purpose by God.

There are many gifts, and also many ways to throw them away. Many Christians get started early in life by loving God and wanting to serve Him with their talents, only to soon see that the world around them seems to value those talents more than the Church, and to be willing to pay for them. There are many good Christians that labor for worldly goods, wasting away their talents for monetary profits that will soon be worthless to them. Matthew 16:26 asks a question that each of us should consider at the start of every day: "For what is a man profited, if he shall gain the whole world, and lose his own soul? Or what shall a man give in exchange for his soul?" God knows that everyone has to make a living, but the question here is, what good will it do you if you live your whole life trying to achieve greatness in this life if you leave no time to serve Him? The Christian must remember not to get side tracked by empty promises by the world around him.

Paul goes on to tell the young preacher, as well as us, that he is to meditate upon the gifts God has given him. Think about them, be thankful for them, develop them, and find better ways to use them. What good does your talent do you if you never use it? We should all carefully consider our talents, and the best way they can be put to use, and then go into action and use them for His glory! There is no excuse for anyone to sit on the sidelines and watch the work of God being done by others. If God didn't have something for you to do today, He would have taken you home yesterday!

Paul goes further by telling Timothy to give himself completely to his gifts. Not to use his gifts for his own profit, as many people are doing today, but just the opposite. The gift you have should drive you to work and serve. Your gift should be moving you to edify others. Many people today waste their entire lives wanting to be or to do something important for the simple fact that their focus is on themselves instead of what God considers important. Matthew 20:16 says, "But it shall not be so among you: but whosoever will be great among you, let him be your minister (servant)." Paul says the outcome of living life this way will be clearly seen by all; "that thy profiting may appear to all." You will profit by serving God, but more importantly, a lost and dying world will profit by it as well!

Lastly, Paul tells the young preacher to take heed unto himself, and unto the doctrine, and continue in them. It is very easy to over extent yourself when you have a goal in mind. It is very easy to begin to let small things into your life that displease the Lord. Paul is warning the Christian here against doing these things. Know your gift, and know the correct way to use it, before you get started. After getting started, be very careful to not begin doing things just for the sake of increase or profit. Again, the reward her is huge; "For in doing this, thou shalt both save thyself, and them that hear thee."

What gift has God blessed you with? Are you using it for personal gain, or for God's glory and honor? God never gifts a person so they can be rich in this life, but so they can be rich in the life to come, and bring others with them.

THE MAN IN THE MIDDLE

1 Timothy 2:5-6, "For there is one God, and one mediator between God and men, the man Christ Jesus; who gave Himself a ransom for all, to be testified in due time."

In this day and time there are many religions out there, and many different ways that a person can choose from to supposedly get to heaven. There are many paths that supposedly lead to a victorious lifestyle, free from all of the things that trouble us on a daily basis. Each religion says that it is either the only correct way, or one of the many ways, to get to heaven. These religions have a lot in common with one another, and have almost one common goal; to have a better life on this earth. These religions are designed by Satan to help people feel good about themselves, and forget about the one problem that supersedes all the others; their sinfulness, and their need for a ransom.

Every other religion on earth today will tell you that you can be good enough to get to heaven on your own. Every other religion today wants you to believe that you don't have a sin problem, or a heart problem, but some disease or other that makes you do the things you do. Every other religion says their either is no fault, or it is someone else's fault. If they can convince you that your sin is not sin, or that someone else is to blame for it, that can ease your feelings of guilt and shame, and they have gained an immense amount of power over you.

But the Word of God says that it is not someone else's fault that you sin. God says that you sin because you have a heart that hates God, and a flesh that wants to glorify itself in the place of God. When you sin, it is because you make yourself and your desires more important than God. Because you have a sinful heart, you cannot know God, cannot feel God, and cannot have a relationship with God. You are destined to live a meaningless life full of loneliness and sinfulness, and die a meaningless death, if you do not have the presence of God in your life.

This is what all of these religions in the world want you to forget. They want you to forget about sin because they do not have the means to remove it. They don't want you to think about God because they cannot offer you the means to know Him. This is what sets Christianity above and beyond all the other religions of this world.

God wants you to know there is a God. God wants you to know that He is God. God wants you to know that you have sinned, and are unable to do anything worthy of having a relationship with Him. He wants you to know that there are requirements and expectations for anyone who hopes to know Him. And He wants you to know that because you cannot meet these requirements and expectations, He has sent someone for you that can.

God has not sent many people to do this work; He has sent only one. God has not developed many ways in which you may be granted access into His presence and into His Heaven; He has made only one Way. God has not given many lives and many chances to find the correct path; this life is the only chance you will ever have. And He has stated very plainly in His Word what this Way is; the man Christ Jesus. Jesus Christ lived in this world as a man so that you and I could have an example of how to live, and a chance to have a relationship with God. Because each of us has sinned, we are unable, of ourselves, to know God. Without knowing Jesus Christ, we will never be able to know God.

Don't be fooled by the religions of Satan! Jesus said in John 14:6, "I am the Way, the Truth, and the Life. No man cometh unto the Father but by me." 2 Corinthians 6:2, "For he saith, I have heard thee in a time accepted, and in the day of salvation have I succoured thee: behold, now is the accepted time; behold, now is the day of salvation."

Have you trusted Jesus Christ for your salvation? If not, He offers you today a chance to know Him. He has given His life, so that you might have life. Put your trust in Him today, because there might not be a tomorrow.

COMFORT FROM ABOVE

2 Corinthians 1:3-4, "Blessed be God, even the Father of our Lord Jesus Christ, the Father of mercies, and the God of all comfort; who comforteth us in all our tribulation, that we may be able to comfort them which are in any trouble, by the comfort wherewith we ourselves are comforted of God."

Many are the times we find ourselves in tribulation in this life. So often, we look at the things we have against us as things that are trying to destroy us. But the fact is that God allows this tribulation into our lives for a specific purpose. This purpose is to grow us. There is two main reasons for trials and tribulations in our lives: either God is trying to get our attention because we have turned from Him into a sinful lifestyle, or God is putting us to the test and trying to increase our trust in Him, and our love for Him. We can also be certain of two things: the devil wants to use what we are going through to destroy us, and God wants to use it to make us better and stronger Christians. The choice is completely ours. One other thing we can be certain of is that the tribulation we face today will determine who we are tomorrow.

When faced with these trials, we first need to examine our hearts, and ask God to show us if there is an area in our lives that He is displeased with. Sometimes we may fall into sin even while trying to live a godly life. This sin is not always obvious. We can be going to church and doing all the right things, and still be out of the will of God! We can have all the right desires and intentions and still be holding part of ourselves from our Lord. When He sees this, He will do whatever He has to do to get our attention. 1 Corinthians 11:31-32, "For if we would judge ourselves, we should not be judged. But when we are judged, we are chastened of the Lord, that we should not be condemned with the world." If we are facing trials in our lives, it may be that God is shaking us so we will take care of the sin in our lives. He loves us too much to allow us to hurt ourselves with unconfessed sin, and to be a hindrance to His plan for ourselves and those in our lives. Everything we do should be measured by the principles of God's Word. If there is anything in our lives that is contrary to Scripture, we are asking for God to allow tribulation into our lives.

If, after examining our own heart and asking God to reveal to us if we are walking contrary to His will, we find nothing, we can approach God with a pure heart and ask Him to show us and teach us what He wants us to learn from our situation. If it is not chastisement we are dealing with, it is a great learning moment that God can use to bring us closer to Him. If we will allow God to work in our hearts, we can be sure that He, not we, will come out victorious through any trial we ever face. Through the pain, through the suffering, through whatever we are facing, God wants us to lean on Him. Proverbs 3:5-6, "Trust in the LORD with all thine heart: and lean not unto thine own understanding. In all thy ways acknowledge Him, and He shall direct thy paths." We may not understand it. It may be completely unfair. But God knows where we will be tomorrow, and He knows the things we need to learn today so that we can make it through tomorrow.

We can be sure that God will let nothing happen in the lives of His children for the purpose of destroying them. We serve a God that can take a broken person today and not only make him a whole person, but even use his broken past as a testimony to bring others into a Christian walk. He will waste no trial or tribulation in our lives!

The things we have learned through leaning upon Him through our trials, He will allow us to help others with. There are people all around us that are hurting and seeking comfort from a world that can offer nothing but destruction. Will you allow Him to bring you through a bumpy path in order than you may show His love to those who have no hope?

REJOICE EVERMORE

Philippians 4:4, "Rejoice in the lord alway: and again I say, rejoice. Let your moderation be known unto all men. The Lord is at hand. Be careful for nothing; but in everything by prayer and supplication with thanksgiving let your requests be made known unto God. And the peace of God, which passeth all understanding, shall keep your hearts and minds through Christ Jesus."

This passage starts out with an extremely hard command for the Christian. Very few, if any of us, can honestly say that we rejoice in the Lord always. And just to make sure we fully understand that he is not just filling space, he repeats it again. Any time we see something repeated in Scripture, we can be sure that what is being said is not just a suggestion. A spirit of rejoicing is vital for the Christian.

When we face life's challenges, our attitude is 95% of the battle. If we go into work with a bad attitude first thing in the morning, we already know it's going to be a terrible day. If we come home from work with a rotten attitude, we can be sure that we will make life miserable, not only for ourselves, but our families as well. If this is true for our professional lives as well as our personal lives, we can be sure it is the same for our spiritual lives. Instead of coming to the Lord in prayer with a defeated mindset, we should enter into His presence with thanksgiving. Psalm 100:4 tells us, "Enter into His gates with thanksgiving, and into His courts with praise: be thankful unto Him, and bless His name." Even in the tough times of life, the Christian has much to be thankful to the Lord for! He has given us eternal life. He has given us victory over sin and death, and He promises that He will never put more on us than we can bear, if we follow Him whole heartedly.

Hebrews 10:19, "Having therefore, brethren, boldness to enter into the holiest by the blood of Jesus." This is yet another reason to rejoice in the Lord no matter how hard life is! Because of the blood of Jesus Christ, and His willingness to take our sins upon Himself, we can enter boldly into the presence of the Almighty God in prayer! We can take our needs, desires, problems, questions, and anything else straight to God, and we can do it with boldness. Before a salvation experience, we could only fear God. We knew we were unworthy and unable to come before Him. Because of the saving grace provided by Jesus, we are no longer enemies to God, but the Scriptures teach us that we are joint heirs with Jesus Christ Himself.

Romans 8:15-17, "For ye have not received the spirit of bondage again to fear; but ye have received the Spirit of adoption, whereby we cry, Abba, Father. The "Spirit itself beareth witness with our spirit, that we are the children of God: and if children, then heirs; heirs of God, and joint-heirs with Christ; if so be that we suffer with Him, that we may be also glorified together." Don't let Satan steel your joy with his lies! He knows that we win or lose by the attitude we go into battle with. Fear and defeat are things the Christian never needs to know! God loved us enough to send His Son to die for us, and His Son loved us enough to be willing to face the horrors of sin and death that He never deserved. Friends, this is love in its truest form! If they loved us enough to do all of this, we can rejoice in not only this, but in the fact that God is willing and able to meet our every need, no matter how big that need may look to us.

"Rejoice in the Lord alway; and again I say, rejoice." No matter the battle you may be facing today, you have a friend that cares for more than anyone ever has. Take your worries and struggles to Him. Let Him fight the battles that you cannot win, because He cannot lose.

THE LIFE LINE

Deuteronomy 10:20, "Thou shalt fear the LORD thy God; Him shalt thou serve, and to Him shalt thou cleave, and swear by His name."

My daughter and I were recently spending a day together, riding and exploring, and came upon a state park with a three level water fall. The first fall was easy to get to, and it wasn't much to look at. It was pretty, but it was also very clear to see that the more beautiful parts were much farther up the side of the mountain. We proceeded to climb to them, up the side of a very steep slope; more of a wall than a hill. In several places there was a rope secured to a tree farther up the slope to give assistance to those wishing to make the journey to the more beautiful parts of the waterfall. I cautioned her against putting all of her faith in the rope, because we had no idea who had placed it there, or how old the rope was.

I immediately began to think about the things in life that people put their faith in; things that seem rock solid, allowing people to fully rest upon them, only to find out after it is too late that they have badly misplaced their trust. Many put their trust in a job, depending on it to give meaning to their life. Sometimes, for several years this will work out fine, but what happens when they get old and have to quit, or when the boss comes to them with news of a cut back? Many lives have been destroyed beyond repair by this news. Some put their trust in their children to give them meaning and enjoyment in life. But sooner or later, the kids will grow up and begin their own life.

For some, it is Church. Countless people today get involved in the Church, thinking this is the way to happiness and fulfillment. While this may be a little better than many others, it is still a terrible mistake when it comes to completely relying upon it. Church leadership may change, or decisions may take place that require the Christian to leave what they have trusted in for many years. Still others get involved in some type of religious clubs, where false teaching is the order of the day. They are deceived into believing that some group knows the only way they should take for the fulfillment they so desire.

There are many paths out there today, and each one of them supposedly go up to that beautiful area we can almost see from our level. Each one may seem sure and solid at the beginning, but how can we know for sure that they don't lead to a dead end that requires us to turn back and start again, or worse yet, that the rope won't break at the time in life that we need it to support our weight the most?

There is only one true, rock solid answer that will never let us down. There is only one true way to find something that will make our lives meaningful. There is only one thing that can fill the emptiness the natural man is always searching to fill. That way is Jesus Christ.

The word fear in this verse speaks of having an awe for something. The Christian should put reverence for God before everything else in life. We should take heed of His warnings and instruction no matter what obstacles we have to endure because of it. The word serve speaks of working for someone. We should hold Jesus Christ above all, and before all. If the world requires that we serve anything else, we should reject what the world has, and serve Christ, no matter the cost. The word cleave speaks of holding to something and refusing to let go. No matter if our families or our friends decide to walk a different path through this life, Scripture tells us to cleave to Christ, and to look to Him to fulfill our dreams and desires. Christ knows what we need way better than we do, and He knows the best way to achieve the goals that He has set before us.

Each day we are given is a new day to put our complete trust in the life line that He has provided. Each day we make the choice to trust in and follow Him, or to trust in the paths that may look easier and have more company on the way. But we can be sure that there is no person in this life that has our best interest in mind than Him, and we can only lose by putting our faith in anything other than Him.

THE SEASONS OF LIFE

Ecclesiastes 3:1, "To every thing there is a season, and a time to every purpose under the heaven."

There are seasons in life that take us to many different places. Some of these seasons are those that everything seems to fall into place and life is easy and enjoyable. These are are the ones we really like, and are often referred to as Mountain Top Experiences. It is during these seasons that the Christian is most likely to lose sight of God. In the midst of the great victories that God Himself has made possible, we bask in the glory of a good life. There are other seasons when life is just very mundane and we are likely to get bored. The everyday tasks seem to never end, and there is very little enjoyment to be found. I have found that it is also easy to loose sight of the Master during these seasons. The work is piled up, and it is easy to neglect our personal time with the Lord. There are still other seasons in life that everything is chaotic and there is not enough time to get all the work done. Looking at these times, we see many times that God has granted us success in what we are doing, but we need to take a step back and see how we can better manage what God has placed before us. For continued success in life, we must learn to be good stewards of not only our money, but also our time and the people that God has placed to help us. This may be friends, family, or fellow members of our church or organization. Then there are the seasons when everything is stormy. As we look around us, we see nothing going right, and nothing but more storms on the horizon. No matter what the storm we may be facing, the outcome could be devastating to one or more areas of our life. It is in these seasons that we learn to trust God the most. We learn more about Him because we must lean upon Him; use His strength to get through the storm. The one thing that all of these seasons have in common is: in every season, we can loose sight of the One who loves us most. The storms may bring us to our knees, but if we are not looking at Him the right way, it will do us no good. In the busy times, we can get too caught up in our work to see Him clearly, and eventually loose sight of Him altogether. In the mundane times, we find it easy to question His love for us. And in the great times, we so often fail to see our need for Him. It is so very important for us to stay focused on the Lord in all times, and in all areas of life. If we are focused on Him in one area, but neglect Him in three others, what good will it do us in the one area. God is a jealous God, and He wants to be number One in all that we do. Life is a learning process, and as we learn, we are sure to make mistakes. But God is willing and able to forgive our mistakes if we will just bring them to Him. No matter what season we find ourselves in, we have a Father in Heaven who loves us, and wants the best for us. He also has a purpose for everything He allows to come into our lives. Let us remember to always look up, and instead of asking why, let us ask, "What do You want me to learn from this?"

A TRUE UNDERSTANDING

Proverbs 20:24, "Man's goings are of the LORD; how can a man then understand his own way?"

In today's world, there is a prevailing attitude that people do not want to be told what to do. They want to be free to "be their own person." They want to make their own decisions, without accepting any input from anyone. It seems that no one wants to be held accountable for their own actions, but everyone wants to hold everyone else accountable.

Many passages in the Old Testament have the words, "Every man did that which was right in his own eyes." This is the world we live in today. It is being taught by many that truth is relative (there are many truths, and my truth may not be the same as yours.) But we can see in Scripture that this idea did not work out well for them then, and it certainly will not work out for us today.

If we go through life looking for our own reasons, doing our own thing, and never considering the cost to others, our lives will be a complete waste, and we will fail in everything we try to do. If we persist in living this way, the cost will be an extremely high body count of our loved ones on the path behind us. Exodus 20:5, "...for I the LORD thy God am a jealous God, visiting the iniquity of the fathers upon the children unto the third and fourth generation of them that hate me." This verse is not saying that God holds the children accountable for the sins of their mother and father. Instead, it is saying that there is a huge consequence for the sins we allow into our lives. This consequence is real, and has much greater effects than we will ever understand.

God tells us that there is a much bigger purpose in life than our fulfillment and pleasure. God shows us through Scripture that He will allow many things into our lives that we may never understand this side of heaven. We will have many opportunities in life to chase our own dreams instead of God's dream for us. If we don't make certain that we have God as the center point in our life, it will be very easy to fall for the lie that we can do whatever we want to do, and if it is wrong, it will not hurt anyone but ourselves.

Many times in life it seems to us that no one understands us. No one understands the struggles we face, the battles we have daily, or the dreams we fear will never be realized in our lives. And while it is true everyone has their own problems and struggles, we should never make the mistake of thinking that there is no one who cares for and understands us. There is One who knows your deepest desires. There is One who loves you more than you have ever been loved before. There is One who understands why you do the things that even you wonder about. There is One who cares so deeply for you that He would, and has, given everything for you.

The Lord Jesus Christ understands you completely. He knows why your mind thinks the way it does. He knows why all of the bad things that have happened to you have happened. He knows how good or bad your past has been, and He has plans to use that past, whatever it is.

Proverbs 3:5, "Trust in the LORD with all thine heart, and lean not upon thine own understanding." When you don't understand, and even when you think you do understand, would you be willing to just give it all up to the Lord? He provides the strength in your times of victory. He is willing to lend you strength in your times of struggling and failing. He will be there to comfort you in times of pain. And He wants to guide you in the midnight times of your life. Trust Him completely with your life. Allow Him to strengthen your faith through the hard times.

OVERCOME TEMPTATION: GOD'S ESCAPE PLAN

1 Corinthians 10:13, "There hath no temptation taken you but such as is common to man: but God is faithful, who will not suffer you to be tempted above that ye are able; but will with the temptation also make a way to escape, that ye may be able to bear it."

This verse reminds us that there is much to be gained by truly understanding the facts about temptation. It often seems that the battles we have with sin and addiction in our lives are problems that we alone face. We all know someone who used to fight the same battles that we struggle with on a daily basis, but have overcome the desire for the thing that once seemed to rule their lives. When looking at this person, we can feel hopeless, helpless, and utter failure. But what we must understand the fact that even though some gain complete victory over some sins in their lives, there are always others that they must fight.

We can understand this more clearly by looking at the life of the greatest missionary that ever lived: the Apostle Paul. In the seventh chapter of the Book of Romans, Paul tells us of his struggle with sin, admitting that the things he wants to do because of his love for God, he neglects to do, and the things he hates, because of his new life in Christ, he ends up doing anyway. It doesn't take any of us long to think back to the last time that we failed to do something that we wanted to do for the Lord, or that we allowed ourselves to go back to after God has given us victory. The sad fact of the matter is simple: this is part of human nature, and every one of us fight this same battle. Though the weapons are different against each of us, the battlefield looks the same for us all.

As we look at others, it is easy for us to think that we are fighting a losing battle that others are not struggling with. But the Word of God tells us that we are not fighting alone! In fact, you are not struggling against anything that every other Christian has not struggled with. Sadly, we are often very good at hiding our problems from those who could have the words that we need to hear for the help that we need. We have been conditioned by the faulty teaching of many preachers and teachers to think that if we struggle with sin, there is something wrong with us. And because of this teaching, many Christians will live their lives in failure, never finding the way to real victory over the sins they struggle so desperately with. Because we often choose to hide our struggles with our Christian family, we not only remove ourselves from the help we need of others, but we also cause others to lose the hope and help they could get from us.

While the beginning of our verse tells us that we each fight the same battle, the rest of the passage gives us a promise that God will provide a way of escape for each and every temptation we are plagued with. These paths of escape are provided by a faithful and loving God, each time we are bombarded by our enemy. The problem is, they are often easy to miss, because we refuse to look them, choosing instead to submit to temptation in order to please our flesh.

While God promises a way of escape, we must be prepared to look for the way He has provided. Sometimes, it is through prayer, while other times it is through removing ourselves from temptation before it ever arrives (don't willingly go to places you know temptation will exist for you). Whatever the way, it is certain that we will not find it if we are not living a life of fellowship with our Savior.

Another path of escape that is often given by our faithful God is the path of encouragement and accountability to others. Proverbs 27:17 tells us that iron sharpens iron (those we choose as friends will influence us); Romans 12:6 tells us that each of us are given different gifts, and that we should use them according to the faith God has given us to use them. Romans 12:5 reminds us that we are all one body in Christ; 1 Corinthians 12:12 tells us that we each are to come together to make one body in Christ.

Friend, are you finding yourself hiding your struggles from others, and wondering why it is that you can't find the escape hatch that has been promised by God? Are you searching for the elusive victory over sin that you have found to be overpowering? Remember that God has promised this way out, but it can only be found and used in the way that He intended. Isn't it time that you stop hiding the parts of you that God wants to change, and the parts that He can use to give others the encouragement they need to find the way of escape in their lives? Open up to the Lord, and let Him use you. Open up to others and let them help you. The way to escape is not in hiding, but in being on the front lines of the battle, where the Lord is waiting!

OVERCOME TEMPTATION: WATCH AND PRAY

Matthew 26:41, "Watch and pray, that ye enter not into temptation: the spirit indeed is willing, but the flesh is weak."

There is much to be said about the temptations we face on a daily basis. Too often we find ourselves in a world of temptation that seems overpowering to us. We want to do the right things, and we love the Lord. We can see the many times in our past that He has protected us, given His grace to us when we didn't deserve it, and has shown us much mercy when He didn't punish us even though we did deserve it. But even while we may think on the love of our Heavenly Father, we choose to turn from Him and His love, and to follow the paths of sin; often even back into the bondage of an addiction that He has given us victory over.

When we are faced with temptation, there are several things we need to remember, and consider. In the next several devotions, we will take a look into temptation: what causes it, why we fight it so much, and what the answer to it is. Why do some fail almost every time they face temptation? Why do others seem to have the ability to withstand it?

First, we must be certain that we are truly a forgiven child of God. There is no way that a person can expect to overcome temptation and addiction in life if they do not have a true relationship with Jesus Christ. Scripture clearly teaches that Jesus is the only way that we can attain forgiveness of our sins, and have a relationship with the Father. Jesus offers this path to forgiveness and restoration, and He offers us a life that can be completely free of the devastating effects of a life lived in bondage. This life can be ours, if only we place our faith and trust in Him, and Him alone.

After a person has come into this relationship offered by the Lord, there are many things that need to be changed and dealt with in order to have a powerful, and fulfilling Christian walk. Our verse for today is an extremely important verse, and we need to carefully consider the thought it provokes. There is a positive and a negative pattern revealed in the first half of the verse: we can watch and pray, and therefore not enter into temptation, or we can neglect to watch and pray, making ourselves easy prey for the enemy.

Christians often wonder why they battle the same things over and over. They fall into sin, come to a point where they seek God's help, only to fall again in a very short while. Many Christians repeat this process throughout their lives, never coming to understand why. It could very well be that they have failed to watch and pray over their lives.

To watch, in this context, is to be vigilant about the areas in our lives that are weak, as well as to know what is going on around us. In this day and age, we have a very watered down idea of what it means to watch. We are so accustomed to watching TV or playing games, but these things are not a true definition of the word "watch." To truly watch means that we are very aware of our surroundings, aware of immediate dangers as well as potential dangers, and that we have a plan in place to protect ourselves against these dangers. Throughout Scripture, we are cautioned to know our strengths and weaknesses, to know the path that God wants us to be on in life, and to be aware of the people we are allowing to shape our lives. It is of the utmost importance to the Christian that we know what it means to watch, and that we keep ourselves around others who will hold us to the standard of the watchful Christian life.

Along with watching, the Christian needs to be praying. We often forget to pray until we find ourselves in need of something from the Lord. We want to live our lives with no duties or responsibilities to hold us back, and praying is just a hindrance when things are all running smoothly for us. But as soon as a problem comes up, we run to God and ask Him to make all things right again. Prayer should be so much more than this! Prayer is the rope that connects our life preserver to the Savior! Having a healthy prayer life will keep us attuned to our Savior, and to His direction for our lives. It will increase our awareness of His love and protection for us, and keep us mindful of the dangers this world has hidden in hard to see places.

Through this verse, we can more clearly see that watching and praying go hand in hand with one another. Look at the end of the verse: "The spirit indeed is willing, but the flesh is weak." Friend, you may be a Christian who loves the Lord and wants to do what is right, but if you are not watching and praying, you will find yourself to be a Christian who wants to live right, without finding the ability to do so. We must have a watchful spirit, and a praying heart, to live victoriously in our Christian life.

OVERCOME TEMPTATION: IN JOY

James 1:2-3, "My brethren, count it all joy when ye fall into divers temptations; knowing this, that the trying of your faith worketh patience."

Last time, we talked about the importance of being watchful and prayerful, and came to the understanding that if we were steadfast in having a watchful attitude with everything in our lives, and if we kept prayer as a priority in our lives, Christ said that we would not fall into temptation. Upon reading these verses, we come to understand that we will, without doubt, have periods of time in our lives that we face temptations. While Matthew 26:41 is true when it says **if** we watch and pray, we will not fall into temptation, it is also true that we will, just as the disciples did, lose our focus from time to time, and forget or neglect to do the things we know we need to do.

James 1:14 tells us exactly why it is that we fall into temptation, and is a verse we must explore. "But every man is tempted, when he is drawn away of his own lust, and enticed." Friends, there is not a person alive today that never struggles with temptation! Satan uses our desires and needs to lure us away, in hopes that we will allow these temptations to seduce us to walk farther and farther away from the loving arms of an Almighty God. He uses the desires of our hearts to pull us away from the only Person who can fulfill those desires to the fullest. He offers low quality, fast food style immediate self-gratification, instead of the slow growing inner fulfillment of realizing these dreams and desires in God's timing, through prayer. He tells us that the quick and easy way he offers is just as good as, or maybe even better than, God's way, and it is very easy for us to fall into his trap.

But there is hope for us, no matter how many times we have fallen for the lies of Satan! Look again at our text; "Count it all joy when ye fall into divers temptations; knowing this, that the trying of your faith worketh patience." No matter what your struggle in this day, you can rest assured that if you will allow God to have His way, He will turn what the enemy has designed for your destruction into not only your victory, but also in your spiritual growth!

Jesus knew when He asked the disciples on that fateful night to watch and pray, that they would, instead, close their eyes and slumber. He also knows that each one of us will do the same on occasion. Just as Jesus used this terrible time of uncertainty in the lives of each of His chosen disciples, He can use this time of struggle and failure in yours! The deciding factor in whether what you and I are struggling with will destroy us or build us up is what we decide to do with it.

Friend, we serve a mighty, and a gracious God. He can turn your destructive addiction or behavior into a testimony that will give Him much glory and honor. He can turn your upside down life right side up again. He can take your broken life and ugly sins and turn them into more completeness and beauty than you have ever thought possible. Instead of letting your temptations draw you away from Him; instead of letting your habits and addictions break your body down and tear your world apart, use them to draw closer to God. Cry out to Him for the strength you know you will never have in your own power! Ask Him to give you wisdom and strength to say no to whatever is tempting you today. He has the power to take your hardest addiction away from you.

Let God use the stumbling block that Satan has thrown at you into a way to make you a stronger and more effective Christian. Today, instead of dreading the hard decisions you must make, take some time to seek God's wisdom and strength before you begin your day. Rise up to meet these struggles with the faith and power of a child of God who has been given overcoming power. Instead of getting discouraged when faced with, and after failing during temptation, "count it all joy....knowing that the trying of your faith worketh patience." Doing this, you can go out and meet your obstacles with confidence and victory, through Jesus Christ!

OVERCOME TEMPTATION: IN LOVE

1 John 2:15-16, "Love not the world, neither the things that are in the world. If any man love the world, the love of the Father is not in him. For all that is in the world, the lust of the flesh, and the lust of the eyes, and the pride of life, is not of the Father, but is of the world."

One of the biggest reasons the Christian finds himself going back into the life of sin that God once gave him victory over is misplaced love. Many of us can think back to the day that God granted us salvation and remember the immediate lifting of burdens that we had been carrying throughout the years. Many of us can also remember the thrill of having been granted victory over a terrible addiction. With these two wonderful things came a deep sense of appreciation and love for our Savior, who was able to give us the things we had been searching for for years. The thought that God would look down on someone who had willingly entered sin and addiction, without the wisdom to know that it would soon become a life draining problem, and give complete victory, is a thought that creates very deep devotion in most people.

But as time goes on, this world has a way of dulling the memories of how great a victory God has freely given us. New problems arise to take the place of old ones. New opportunities are also a part of a new life in Christ. As the Lord takes some things out of our lives, He always replaces them with new and improved things, simply because He loves us and wants the best for us. It is our responsibility to keep fresh in our mind the things He has done for us. If we begin to take for granted the freedom that has been given, we can very soon find that freedom lost to us, exchanged for the old lifestyle we once lived and couldn't find our way out of.

Even as we live a Christian life, it is very easy to fall out of a loving relationship towards our Heavenly Father. In Revelation 2, we can find Jesus talking to the Church of Ephesus. He acknowledges the fact that they are outwardly living a godly life, and also the fact that they use Scripture to check up on those who claim to be leaders of the Church. But in verse four, Jesus tells them what He has against them: They have left their first love. Friend, this is a very real and serious problem and possibility for the Christian to have, and one that is extremely hard to correct once we have fallen into it. The only cure for it is for the Christian to repent, and to return to the first works, or to remember the victory that has been granted, and to get back to the love that we felt for the Savior when we were first saved.

Our text cautions us in the three areas that can pose a problem for us: the lust of the flesh, the lust of the eyes, and the Pride of life. We must be constantly aware of these desires in our lives! If we ignore them, or miss their presence in our thoughts, the results can quickly become devastating to us. The lust of the flesh is a desire for the pleasure of the outward senses, whether taste, smell, or touch. This lust will draw us in to many of our past sins if we allow it to take root in our life. This lust comes from our fleshly needs, and can very quickly become overpowering to us. The lust of the eyes is a desire for pleasure of imagination; wanting things that are wonderful, new, and beautiful. We all like nice things, but the desire for these things can very quickly draw us into a life of sin and bondage. The pride of life is a desire for a position that brings honor and praise from others.

Every sinful desire that the Christian can find himself battling takes its root in one of these lusts. Every sinful desire that the Christian can submit to in life first has to come as the Christian begins to forget what great things the Savior has done for him. We must always remember the great love that Christ has shown to us, and the great forgiveness He has displayed to us. We each make decisions on a daily basis as to how we will react to the problems and opportunities we have. Will we allow the grace and freedom God has given us to lead us back into bondage to sin, or will we choose to keep looking at our Lord in love? Friend, while we cannot lose our salvation, we can certainly give away our joy, our victory, and our love for the Savior. Will you choose today to love the world, or to love the Lord?

OVERCOME TEMPTATION: SUBMITTING TO GOD

James 4, 7-8, "Submit yourselves therefore to God. Resist the devil, and he will flee from you. Draw nigh to God, and He will draw nigh to you. Cleanse your hands, ye sinners; and purify your hearts, ye double minded."

The times the Christian finds that he struggles with temptation the most, and loses the fight the most, will be the times that he has not been submitting to God. For sure, every Christian struggles with temptation and sin in their lives on a daily basis, and we all make wrong choices from time to time. But if you are living a lifestyle of defeat, you will probably find that there is at least one area in your life that you have refused to submit to God in. Many Christians will find that they ask God to deliver them from sin or addiction, but have "hidden" sins in their lives that they want to keep out of God's control. They find themselves wondering why God will not help them or protect them, but refuse to see that the fault lies not with God, but in their own hearts.

Sometimes, Christians even find themselves blaming God for putting them into situations they find themselves in. James 1:13 tells us that God cannot be tempted with evil, and that He will never tempt someone to do evil. Many times we find ourselves in situations where we are being tempted, and wonder how we got where we are. Again, we can be sure that God had nothing to do with it: we simply cannot blame Him for the messes we make.

While we cannot expect God to come and save us from temptations while we are living a life of refusal to His will, He does make us some fantastic promises, if we will live according to His plan for our lives. Our text tells us to submit ourselves to God. This is the first decision we must make if we want to see spiritual victory in our lives. While we so often try to make ourselves believe that we can live for ourselves without answering to anyone, Scripture makes it very clear to us that as humans, we will serve someone. We cannot live for ourselves! If we refuse to submit to God, we are choosing to submit to Satan!

Along with this submission to God comes resisting the devil. God makes it possible for us resist this great enemy, and overcome him. So many people try to fight an enemy they cannot see, and who is much smarter than they are, and lose time after time simply because they have no idea how to win over him. But if we will put God in His rightful place in our hearts, He will be in a position make this fight for us. He will give us the strength to resist our enemy in the areas that we have never had strength before. He will give us wisdom, and will guide us, leading us away from battles we could never hope to win, 1 Corinthians 10:13. He will give us the power to resist our enemy, and He promises that if we resist him, he will flee from us!

The next thing the Christian must do is to draw nigh to God. Our Lord is the almighty God, and He can do anything He wants to do, but He will never force you to be close to Him. He leaves this decision up to you, and you alone. He is right where He has always been, waiting on you to draw towards Him. If you will reach out for Him, you can be sure that you will find His loving hand. Not only will He make sure that you find Him, but He will then draw you, because He knows that you cannot do it alone.

Next, our text tells us to cleanse our hands, and to purify our hearts. Scripture tells us that God cannot and will not coexist with sin. Even after the Christian has drawn towards God, he can undo everything that has been done, the minute he allows sin to have place in his heart again. That sin that we want to hide from God, no matter how small it is, will be the very sin that causes us to leave God's protective power over our lives. We must keep our hands and hearts clean. We will sin, and we will make bad choices in life, but if we want God's blessing and power, we must confess and forsake those little things as soon as God brings them to our attention. God can and will help us to battle and overcome temptation, sin, and addictions in our lives, but we must be willing to stay submitted to Him in every area of our lives. As soon as He shows us something that He is not happy with, and we refuse to take the actions necessary to get rid of it, we are choosing to begin submitting to Satan, and a holy and righteous God will never share a room in our heart with the devil.

Are you finding that no matter how much you try to resist temptation, you lose the fight? Look in your heart and see who it is that you have been living in submission to. By yourself, you have no chance of winning the fight you are struggling to win; with God in His rightful place on the throne of your heart, you will find that you have already won the war!

THE BREAKER OF DECEPTION

Ephesians 4:7, "But unto every one of us is given grace according to the measure of the gift of Christ."

So often in the life of a young Christian, or a Christian of many years who has not grown in the knowledge of Christ, we face problems and/or sins that are very hard to overcome. To us, the issue may seem impossible to conquer; so many times we just ignore it in our lives. It is left to fester, grow, and overflow into all areas of life. Sometimes it is a relatively small thing, but something that we have grown attached to. Whatever it is in your life, you have to come to the point that you are willing to give it up to Him.

God never reveals a sin to us that He will accept our ignoring. He never allows a problem to come to us that He wants us to just sweep under the rug and forget. These things are very much part of the growing process of our Christian walk. If we ignore them when He reveals them, our growth doesn't just stop; it goes backward. No person can just stay where he is at in life. There is only one constant; that is God Himself. All others are constantly in motion. This means that when we stop growing due to ignoring something He wants from us, we start going backwards in our walk with Him, and in our personal life.

It is satan himself that wants us to believe that we can just keep something unpleasing to God in our lives. It is always him that wants us to allow the little stuff to remain. It is always him that tells us something will be too hard for us. It is always him that wants us to go to door number two.

But God gives grace for us to change. God gives help when we cannot go any further. God has already overcome these things in life that keep getting us down, and He offers us His power to change. Some of the ways He offers this can be found in verses 11-12, "And He gave some, apostles; and some, prophets; and some, evangelists; and some, pastors and teachers; for the perfecting of the saints, for the work of the ministry, for the edifying of the body of Christ." We must not only surround ourselves with those walking the same way we want to go; we must listen when God talks through them. God has placed these people in our path to help guide us. Even when they say those things we don't want to hear, we must open our ears and listen. God has these Christian workers, not to make us uncomfortable, but for the edifying of the Church.

What is it that God wants to change in your life? What have you been holding back from Him? What have you been trying to hide? What have you been making excuses for keeping hold of? He cannot take you farther in your walk with Him until you give Him all. No matter how important this sin is to you, give it up to the One who loved you enough to die for you. Make Him the most important thing in life, and He will give you grace to turn loose of the sins that are dear to you.

Verse 14 continues, and gives us the reason for the grace He gives to us, "That we henceforth be no more children, tossed to and fro, and carried about with every wind of doctrine, by the sleight of men, and cunning craftiness, whereby they lie in wait to deceive."

God wants to give us grace to break the deception we have lived under. Will you take it?

THE FAVOR OF GOD

2 Samuel 15:25-26, "And the king said unto Zadok, Carry back the Ark of God into the city: if I shall find favour in the eyes of the LORD, He will bring me again, and shew me both it, and His habitation: But if He thus say, I have no delight in thee: behold, here am I, let Him do to me as seemeth good unto Him."

These words were spoken by King David shortly after his son, Absalom, stole the kingdom from him. David was the strongest king Israel would ever know, as well as the king who was hand-picked by God to lead the nation of Israel. His was the right of leadership, with an army to enforce the kings desires. As well as being a man after God's own heart, who certainly had favor with God.

Yet, instead of fighting for his rights and position, he threw himself upon God's mercy. He would not fight for what he thought was his rightful place. He chose to make himself humble, ask God to restore his place if God still wanted him there.

So often we perceive wrongdoing on the parts of others toward us. If someone has favor in the eyes of the boss at work, we consider them to be our enemy. If someone receives special treatment over us, we envy them, and hold bitterness towards them. We tend to see only one sided when it comes to ourselves verses anyone else. We see all areas we are more qualified than everyone else. We see all our qualities, and many times way overstate them. And we like to look for every little fault of everyone around us, pointing out, at least to ourselves, why we are better and more qualified than they are.

But God tells us to be humble. God teaches us in Philippians 2:3, "Let nothing be done through strife or vainglory; but in lowliness of mind let each esteem other better than themselves." When we do anything or fight for anything just because we think we "deserve" it, God says it is sin. We should never compare ourselves to our neighbor! If we want to compare with someone, we should look at Jesus Christ as the bar to which all others should try to reach.

When we look at Jesus, and His goodness, gentleness, love, and meekness, even unto the death of the Cross, we will every one fall woefully short. But once we begin looking to Him as the benchmark of life, we will begin to see the changes in our lives that we so desperately need. And, once we start getting this right, we will begin to see the good traits in those around us instead of only the shortcomings.

In short, once we start getting this right, the Lord himself will start opening doors in life for us, because when we humble ourselves, He says He will lift us up. Instead of trying in vain to find favor in the eyes of unjust men who are after only their gain, wouldn't it be much better to try to find favor in the eyes of the One who didn't consider His own gain, but gave His life so that we could gain Life?

THE LORD MY ROCK

2 Samuel 22:2-4, "And he said, the LORD is my rock, and my fortress, and my deliverer; The God of my rock: in Him will I trust: He is my shield, and the horn of my salvation, my high tower, and my refuge, my Saviour; Thou savest me from violence. I will call on the LORD, who is worthy to be praised: so shall I be saved from mine enemies."

King David spoke these words after God displayed His mighty power in his life, and upon his kingdom. King David, the most powerful king of the nation of Israel, looked upon God as his strength and power. David knew that all that he had was given to him by an all-powerful God. Any good thing that came into his life was directly from the mercy and grace of God. David had been through terrible things in his life. He spent years hunted by the previous king of Israel. He spent many years of his life on the run, at times hiding out among the very enemies of Israel. He had failed many times throughout his life, costing his family, as well as his kingdom, many thousands of lives. Yet he still looked upon God as a God of grace and mercy; a God who delivers; a God who saved him from violence.

All of us can look back on our lives and remember well the hard and dangerous times; the times that almost cost us our lives and our families; times that may have cost us our jobs and our happiness. All of these things are very much a part of our lives. Many of us are going through these times right now. We can choose to approach them in one of two ways.

The first, and often deadly way to approach them, is by looking to God as the cause of our problems. How many times I have heard family members and friends blame their hardships on God, and turn farther from the very One that can help. They refuse to accept the blame for things they have done in their lives. They want to believe that God is the very cause of their pain. This approach can only end in more hardship and sadness.

The second approach, and the one God longs for us to use, is the one that puts Him in His rightful place as Lord and Savior of our lives. It is true that God lets terrible things come into our lives; but it is never true that He allows these things in to destroy us. His very purpose in letting us face these terrible times in life is to get us to look at the One that has the answers. He loves us so much that He would do anything to make us open our eyes.

We are prideful creatures. Often, we have to be humbled by God, because we refuse to humble ourselves. We want to be the god of our lives, and make terrible choices, just as King David made many, bringing the judgment of God upon ourselves. But even in judgment, God is merciful and gracious. In the midst of judgment, if we will but turn to Him, He will help us in our time of greatest need. If we will turn to Him, putting our complete trust in His goodness, even during these times, we will be able to say, as David did, God is my rock; my fortress; my deliverer; my shield; the horn of my salvation; my strength!

Just as David learned, so can we also, that God wants the very best for us. He wants this for us so badly that He is very willing to use terrible things to get us to turn to Him. But it doesn't have to be after the hardships of life that we learn this. We can choose to turn to Him before He has to go to these extreme measures.

Matthew 23:12 tells us, "And whosoever shall exalt himself shall be abased; and he that shall humble himself shall be exalted." God wants us to acknowledge Him as our very source of life. The choice is ours. Will you look to God today as your Rock, or will you choose to ignore Him? In looking to him, He will save you from your biggest enemy: yourself.

THE MANY FACES OF GOD

2 Samuel 22: 26-28, "With the merciful Thou wilt shew Thyself merciful, and with the upright man Thou wilt shew Thyself upright. With the pure Thou wilt shew Thyself pure; and with the forward Thou wilt shew Thyself unsavoury. And the afflicted people Thou wilt save: but Thine eyes are upon the haughty, that Thou mayest bring them down."

There are so many people in our lives that irritate us; so many that make life harder than it should be for us. There are many with us in this life that we look at and think, "My life would be so much simpler without you." There are those who would do us harm, or at least be happy about our misfortunes and hardships in life. And it is very easy to think and act in a negative manner towards them—unless we take heed to these verses in Scripture.

God clearly teaches us in Scripture that we should treat others the way we would want to be treated. He doesn't tell us to do right to others if they do right to us; instead, to do right to others no matter how they do to us. Most of the people we run across in life that treat us badly need a touch from God desperately, even if they don't understand it. Even many Christians have become this way because they have rejected His teachings and ignored His warnings.

But we don't have to return ugliness with ugliness. We can choose to be salt and light in a dark world that has lost its savior! One of the quickest ways we can do this is to simply show the love of Christ to the world around us; let them see the difference that He is making in our lives. We were probably once just like this, and but by the grace of God, would still be.

But even if we are not motivated to do good to others because we love them and seek their gain through Christ, we would do well to remember that one day we will stand before God and give answer for the way we have treated others. If we show mercy to this world, God says He will show mercy to us. But if we return hatefulness and selfishness to those who give us the same, we can expect to find the judgment of God upon us as well.

We find the Lord's Prayer in Matthew 6:9-13. In it, He teaches us to pray for His will to be done on earth. We are instructed to pray for Him to provide our needs for the day, as well as to ask His forgiveness, as we have forgiven others who have wronged us. How can we really pray for His will to be done, and then go out and directly violate it? How can we ask Him to provide for our needs when we refuse to show others the true love of God that they need? And how can we expect Him to forgive us for our wrongdoing every day when we insist on giving justice to those in our lives that do us wrong?

God is truly willing to do all those things found in the Lord's Prayer for us. But He expects us to take His mercy and grace and not keep it for ourselves, but show it to the world. Matthew 7:2, "For with what judgment ye judge, ye shall be judged: and with what measure ye mete, it shall be measured to you again."

Let us not just find the forgiveness of a wonderful, loving God; but let us give it to those around us that desperately need it. Once we do this, we will find the great blessings of God falling around us too quickly to count them all.

CHAMPION COMPLAINERS

Exodus 14:11-12, "And they said unto Moses, Because there were no graves in Egypt, hast thou taken us away to die in the wilderness? Wherefore hast thou dealt thus with us, to carry us forth out of Egypt? Is not this the word that we did tell thee in Egypt, saying, Let us alone, that we may serve the Egyptians? For it had been better for us to serve the Egyptians, than that we should die in the wilderness."

We find the nation of Israel in these verses with the army of Pharaoh behind them, with the intention of taking them back into bondage, and the Red Sea before them, blocking their way of escape from an army they could not possibly defeat. There is no doubt that as they looked behind them at their powerful enemy, and looked before them at an impassible obstical, their minds were filled with fear over what would happen next. They started a habit very early in their walk with God that would follow them for many, many years.

They knew very well who was leading them out of bondage to Egypt. They had been praying for years that God would deliver them. They knew the promises that were made to Abraham, Isaac, and Jacob. God had shown His power over situations much worse than the one they were now facing, but instead of trusting Him to prove Himself again, they decided to complain. They started a habit that would have devastating consequences for them, and their nation, for the thousands of years between that day and now.

Almost immediately after God delivered them from Pharaoh by dividing the Red Sea, they complained about being thirsty, and God provided water for them. Then only days after this, they complained about not having enough to eat, and God provided for them again. Time after time, we can read of how Israel complained about Moses and God, and time after time we can read of how God provided what they were wanting. God finally tired of it and judged Israel harshly.

There is much to be learned by the Christian through this story. It is very easy for us to complain when we are uncomfortable; when things don't go just the way we want them to go. It is very easy to lose our zeal for serving God when life begins to get hard. This is just what our enemy wants. Instead, we would do well to remember some things.

First, we should remember who it is that we serve. We serve the God of creation! We serve the One who could have condemned us to eternal separation from Him in a Lake of Fire that burns forever. We serve a God that has never met a situation He could not control; indeed, He has never met a situation He has not allowed. When we face opposition that is far more powerful than we are, as Israel faced on the banks of the Red Sea, we should remind ourselves that God just may be getting to show the world around us His power and glory.

Second, we should remember that God has promised us anything that we need. We have the awesome privilege of serving a God who has promised us that He will provide our needs, no matter what those needs are. Time after time we can see these promises in Scripture. He will never put us somewhere that He is not capable of taking care of us in. The nation of Israel, had they put and kept their trust in God, could have never failed. Something so simple for them was overlooked by them; all they had to do was ask Him for provision. This simple thing is also very often overlooked by God's people today. It seems that many Christians would much rather complain about what they don't have than to just ask God for what they need.

Third, we should remember that God brings discomfort into our lives for two reasons: either because He is trying to grow us, or because we have sinned. Every situation Israel found themselves in were for one of these two reasons. God took them through the wilderness because He knew they couldn't go the other way because of a strong enemy. He knew their faith would fail in the face of such a force. When we find ourselves facing a wilderness period, we should understand that maybe God is trying to build our faith with smaller battles than we would have faced by going the direct route. In these times, we should also examine our hearts to see if there is any hidden sin in our lives that God is chastising us for.

Lastly, we need to remember that God will tire of hearing us complain to Him, and about Him. God gave Israel many chances to accept what He was trying to do in their lives. At first, He lovingly corrected them, gently opening their eyes and hearts to the fact that He was their God, and wanted them to trust and follow Him, no matter where the path led, or how rough it became. Finally, because they refused to learn from the gentle correction, there was nothing left by stern correction.

Are you going through the wilderness right now? If not, I assure you that you soon will. God has seen fit to let us see the mistakes that His chosen people made, and learn from them. God wants His people to trust and follow Him, no matter what happens. He wants us to lean on Him and depend upon Him. He wants us to stop complaining about what He is doing in our lives, and just ask Him for the strength and provision to let Him have His way.

THE TRUE VICTOR

Exodus 14:14, "The LORD shall fight for you, and ye shall hold your peace."

Many times Christians enter the battle field of life looking at the power of the enemies we have stacked up against us. When we enter the fight with this in our thoughts, we have nothing to do but be defeated. Our enemy is so powerful, so bold, so unashamed, and is constantly able to surround us with things we just cannot win against.

Our enemy knows our weakness. Our enemy knows all about our past. Our enemy knows our fears. How can we meet him in battle? The answer is so simple that we often overlook it. We try to meet an unstoppable foe with fleshly weapons. But these weapons are designed by the enemy himself. They are made to look good, strong, and capable so we will be drawn to use them instead of the weapon that will always win.

God cannot lose. He has always been, and will always be, the victor. No matter the conflict. No matter what weapon the enemy chooses to use against us, the LORD tells us to hold our peace. Nothing we can do will be enough except this very thing. We must put our trust in Him. He wants to fight our battles for us. When things look the worst, God is at His best. The enemy has our defeat in mind, but God has our growth and protection as priority.

Just as Elisha, at Dothan, saw the LORD's protection and knew he would be safe, through the eyes of faith we can see the same. The world will hate us if we love and serve God. They will try to hinder us, hurt us, even kill us. What does it matter?

Do we really realize whom it is that we serve? His work will go on. His plans will not be stopped, no matter what tries to get in the way. Put your trust in Him. Let Him fight for you today.

FORWARD BY FAITH

Exodus 14:15-16, "And the LORD said unto Moses, Wherefore criest thou unto me? Speak unto the children of Israel, that they go forward: But lift thou up thy rod, and stretch out thine hand over the sea, and divide it: and the children of Israel shall go on dry ground through the midst of the sea."

There are many times that we find ourselves at a dead end in life. What we thought was the path that would lead to success and fulfillment turns out to be a lie. Sometimes we look out and see ourselves surrounded by the enemy, with no place to get away, and putting up a fight will certainly lead to complete failure. Or maybe what should have been the correct direction in life has been destroyed by personal decisions that were wrong. Whatever the reason, as the Christian looks at what he is up against, there seems to be no options left.

This is where the nation of Israel found themselves in this verse. They were surrounded by the enemy on one side and an impassable body of water on the other side. As they cried out to God, and questioned Him, they had lost all hope for their dreams of having their own land. For hundreds of years, they had been in slavery to the nation of Egypt. For hundreds of years they had told about the promises of God to their forefathers about making them a blessed people. Now, on the brink of seeing these dreams come to pass, they were watching them vanish into thin air.

When you find yourself in this situation, the first thing you want to do is question God. Are the promises nothing but lies? Is He really the God He claims to be? Does He care about you, or are you just entertainment to Him as He sits up in Heaven watching your world crumble around you?

We can see in this verse that the Lord asked Moses a very simple question. Why are you crying out to me? At first glance, it appears very obvious why Moses cried out for God to intervene in their situation. It looked as if they would all be destroyed that day. But upon further meditation of the Lord's question to Moses, it becomes understandable why God asked this question. God had given them promises of protection. He had promised to provide to them the things they needed. He had promised them a land of their own. He had promised them He would make a great nation from them. If they had really believed His words, they would not be questioning Him at all. They would have known that somehow He would get them out of the trouble they were facing.

If we are completely honest with ourselves, we would have to admit that most of the time the true problems in our life come because we do not trust God with His promises to us. Maybe the situation we find ourselves in today is a very uncomfortable one, but the chances are great that we have created this situation because of our unbelief.

We, as Israel, know what God has promised to us. He has given us direction; have we followed it? He has promised to provide; are we struggling against Him because we do not like what He has provided? He has promised to give protection from the enemy; are we going around His protective hands because we love the things of the world more than the things of God? He has promised to come back for His Church and make a new, eternal home for His people; have we decided that we would rather live in this world of strife and chaos because of the pleasures it offers?

You see, we can have one or the other, but we cannot have both. Many times the Christian makes the excuse that he is waiting on God to answer a prayer, when God has already given the answer. Maybe it's time to stop crying out to God because we are unhappy in a circumstance, and just move on in faith. God has promised these things to us already; maybe while we are waiting on Him to answer, He is waiting on us to pick up the shield of faith and move forward.

GOD, THE LOVER AND PROVIDER

Exodus 16:8, "And Moses said, this shall be, when the LORD shall give you in the evening flesh to eat, and in the morning bread to the full: for that the LORD heareth your murmurings which ye murmur against Him: and what are we? Your murmurings are not against us, but against the LORD."

Every time I read or think about the nation of Israel, I wonder how in the world they could have been so blind to God's provision, protection, and love. Those first steps out of the slavery to Egypt were very nervous steps for them. But they quickly found that God did their fighting for them. God provided a safety net and the ultimate form of security. Nothing could get past or through Him. But still they complained constantly. Nothing was good enough for them. They were hungry, and God fed them. They were thirsty, and God gave them water to drink. Not just every now and again, but every time they were in need. But soon, the very blessings given by God were taken for granted, and they complained yet again. Instead of asking for what they needed, they wanted to go back to their old life. How could they be so blind? How could they not see God's hand in every aspect of their lives? How could they murmur against a God that loved them so much?

It is easy to look at others and see their faults and failures. It is easy to pick their lives apart and see how, when, where, and why they fail. It is so very hard to see how we do the same things in life today though. When God blesses us with undeserved affections, giving us the things we dreamed of, we can clearly see Him in our lives, and praise Him. When He gives us a mighty victory in some area of our live, we love Him so much. But the very next time that something goes wrong, or just goes other that the way we planned, we find ourselves questioning His love for us. We question His ability to give us provision. We question His faithfulness. Many times we may even question His existence.

How can we, His people, bought by His very blood, stoop down to this level? How can we question anything about Him? He has proved His love and power to change us. He has proved over and over His willingness to heal our wounds. He has proved His power time after time to bring us back to Him when we go astray. How can we question Him?

Could it be that we are just like these people that we like to look at and point out where they were wrong? And could it be that we are wrong for the very same reasons that they were wrong? Their very lack of loving and just willingly following Him led to every set back they ever had. Have our setbacks and failures come to us for the same reasons? It is a lack of faith...but "faith cometh by hearing, and hearing by the Word of God." Love comes from being devoted to someone, and devotion comes from spending time with and getting to know someone.

You see, in their world, they had not received the promised Deliverer yet. They had a kind of blind faith, looking forward to something that would never come in their lifetimes. We, on the other hand, look back to a Savior who has already willingly given everything for us. They had only a promise. We have a history Book given to us by God that proves His love for us.

The problem and lack of faith is far greater on our side of the Cross than it was on theirs.

When we find ourselves short on faith, it is apparent that we have not spent enough time with the God who loved us enough to give everything for us, even His life. When we question Him, it is because we don't know Him enough. He has given us everything we need to fix these problems in our lives. He wants a relationship with us more than anything, just like He did with Israel.

BODLY COME TO HIM

Hebrews 4:14-16, "Seeing then that we have a great high priest, that is passed into the heavens, Jesus the Son of God, let us hold fast our profession. For we have not an high priest which cannot be touched with the feeling of our infirmities: but was in all points tempted like as we are, yet without sin. Let us therefore come boldly unto the throne of grace, that we may obtain mercy, and find grace to help in time of need."

Many people life a life of defeat and failure while trying to do the right things the whole time simply because they do not follow the advice of this passage. For some reason, we have the idea that God is untouchable to us. If we have made mistakes, He will have nothing to do with us. Maybe because we have fallen again and again in the same area, or areas, we feel that He does not want us anymore.

While it is true that God hates sin, especially in the life of a Christian, He offers forgiveness to us, if only we will come to Him and ask. We do not serve a God that is looking for a reason to abandon us. If that was the case, He would never have sent His Son to die for us. He had, and has, every reason in the world to condemn each and every one that has ever taken a breath.

Instead, He is looking for a reason to forgive us. He sent His Son. He gave us His law. He shows us mercy and grace on a daily basis. He tells us that His mercies are new every morning. He allows us to live, many times with sin in our lives, so He can woo us back to Him through His mercy and grace. He gives us help when we ask for it. He gives us strength when we need it.

He has become our high priest that loves us, and has shown us His willingness to do whatever it takes to bring us into fellowship with Him. Because we cannot ever be good enough to earn our way into heaven, or strong enough to stay on the path, He provides the way, and keeps us on the path. This is why we should, and how it is possible for us to hold fast our profession. He has been tempted in every way possible, yet without sin, and He offers us His power over sin.

For this reason, we can boldly approach the throne with our prayers, our needs, our desires, and our weaknesses. We can trade in a life of defeat and failure for a life of victory and discipline. The power is there to help us overcome any sin we might be battling with. He loves us. He wants to help us. He holds the door open and begs us to come to Him for help. But He will not force us.

What are you battling with today? What do you need help with today? He is waiting for you to come to Him and ask. The choice is up to you.

CLOUD OF ENCOURAGEMENT

Hebrews 12:1, "Wherefore seeing we also are compassed about with so great a cloud of witnesses, let us lay aside every weight, and the sin which doth so easily beset us, and let us run with patience the race that is set before us."

This verse comes directly after what most of us know as "The Great Faith Chapter" of the Bible. Chapter 11 of Hebrews talks about the men and women of great faith that did many great works for the Lord. In Chapter 11, we see that God chose to use many people who were very small, unknown people to do the mighty works for Him. These men and women had many problems in their lives that had to be dealt with before God could use them like He did; problems that only God could help them through. Many of them had great sins that had to be dealt with; but with God's power, even the stumbling blocks laid by Satan had no power to stop these great people of faith.

Chapter 11 is a wonderful chapter of encouragement given to us by our Savior. The Christian can see here that the Lord has a plan, and where He has a plan, He has made a way to achieve that plan. God has told us the stories, and the failures, of these people because He wants us to understand that nothing is too hard for Him to overcome. It does not matter what sin you struggle with; God can and will give you the strength to overcome the stronghold you deal with in your life. Chapter 11 is the faith chapter; chapter 12 goes on to tell the struggling Christian how he can also be a person of faith.

First, our passage says to lay aside every weight. Not all things the Christian struggles with are sin. There are many good things in this world that are not necessarily godly things. There are wonderful causes a Christian could get involved in that are not ungodly, but they will hinder a full Christian life. If you have a house full of teenagers that are all involved in three different sports, there will be no time left for serving God. These things are what Scripture refers to as weights, and they should be laid aside. God knows we want to be part of our communities, and that we want our children to enjoy their childhood years; but we should put strict limits upon the things that weigh us down and hinder us from living a life for Christ.

Next, the Christian should lay aside the sin which so easily besets him. Many people think of this sin as the "big sin" they struggle with. They think that if they can get victory over that one area in life, life will go right, and they will become godly people. The truth is, you will never keep the victory over the "big sins" in your life if you do not learn to keep the "small sins" out of your life. That sin that so easily besets you is that little thing that can go unnoticed by those around you. That almost invisible sin you try to get by with is what opens the door to bigger and greater sins. The Christian who wants to walk with Christ in victorious living must first learn to give Christ those pet sins that most people do not even consider sins.

After the Christian learns to lay aside the things that weigh him down in life and give up those "small sins," he must learn to run. If you have spent much time running at all, you know the very thought requires discipline. The body does not want to run; you must force it. The body wants to go the path of least resistance; you must follow the trail cut out of the mountain of life by God. The body wants to rest; you must push it to go the next step.

And not only must the Christian run, but he must run with patience. Not everything in life will work out like you want it to. You will slip and fall along the path that God has laid out for you. People will disappoint you. People will challenge you. You will find constant resistance to what God wants to do in your life by your own sin nature. You must learn to love and trust God through it all. You must have the final goal in mind to overcome the stumbling blocks your enemy has set in your path.

Although the path God has put you on may look impossible, you have a great cloud of witnesses that prove to you that it is very possible, with God's help and direction for your life.

FOCUS ON THE KING

Hebrews 12:2, "Looking unto Jesus the author and finisher of our faith; who for the joy that was set before Him endured the cross, despising the shame, and is set down at the right hand of the throne of God."

In our last devotion, we learned that Scripture tells us to lay aside every weight, the sin that easily besets us, and that we are to run with patience the race that God has put us in. We have many godly examples in God's Word of people who have done this, and we see how God has used them for His glory and honor. We also know how impossible of a task this is to do day in and day out. Many times we get started on the right path, but lose our way very quickly, back in to our old habits and sins.

This verse tells the Christian how to accomplish the tasks set before him in verse one. The only way you and I can hope to fulfill the commands in verse one is to look unto Jesus. Jesus is the only example of how to do these things perfectly. In His lifetime, He had perfect time management, showed perfect skills of separating Himself from people, places, and things that were trying to weigh Him down, consistently refused to sin when attacked with temptation, and had perfect patience throughout His ministry on this earth. He, and He alone, can help the Christian live a victorious life, free from the bondage of sin and addiction.

The Christian must look at Jesus Christ when in the midst of life's storms. We can take example from Peter's experience of walking, then sinking, upon the stormy sea in Matthew 14:22-32. Just as Peter had the faith to begin his walk upon the water, knowing he had been called by Christ, so many of us have begun this impossible walk to Jesus' side. But Peter's eyes soon began to see the boisterous waves, instead of the God-Man. He soon felt the wind upon his face, making it hard to take a breath. You see, as long as he kept Jesus in focus, he never knew about what was happening around him. But as soon as he began taking notice of the dangerous situation he was in, he completely forgot that he was doing something that only two men in the history of the world have ever done.

If we want to live a clean life in this dirty world, we are going to have to look at the One who can make us walk on it, instead of in it. We must spend time with Him in prayer and in the reading and study of the Word of God. We must spend our days with the understanding that He is with us, just as He was with Peter. We must make time to meditate upon His Word, and practice His presence in our lives. He will give us the strength to endure the temptations we face daily, if only we allow Him to walk with us.

So often, we rush through the morning, at best just reading a few verses, and then run off to work, leaving Jesus at home until we return to rush through the next morning's reading. But when we do this, we set ourselves up for failure! Each one of us is only human; we each battle our own sins. We need help in fighting this battle. We are going to have our eyes focused upon something; we are going to serve something; we are going to meditate upon something. If you do not determine to focus on, meditate upon, and serve Jesus Christ this morning, where will you find yourself tonight?

Jesus Christ knows your struggles. He knows the weights that are trying to pull you under the stormy see in which you are travelling today. He knows the temptations that your enemy will set before you today, trying to blindside you right back into a lifestyle of sin. And He wants you to set your eyes upon Him, and let Him deal with each stumbling block in your path. He is your only hope of walking untouched by the enemy in this life. Keep your focus upon Him, and He will guide you through the obstacle course of life.

"Turn your eyes upon Jesus, look full in His wonderful face, and the things of earth will grow strangely dim, in the light of His glory and grace," —song lyrics written by Helen H. Lemmel.

CONSIDER CHRIST

Hebrews 12:3-4, "For consider Him that endured such contradiction of sinners against Himself, lest ye be wearied and faint in your minds. Ye have not yet resisted unto blood, striving against sin."

Yesterday we talked about the fact that we are to look at Jesus, keeping Him in focus always, above and beyond all the struggles we have in in life. He is the author and finisher of our faith. The only victory we will ever hope to have in life can only be found in Him. He alone has the power and wisdom to guide us through this life. He alone has the ability to keep us from going back into a life of sin and destruction.

It is only when we get our eyes off of Jesus Christ that sin can become dominant in our life. No, the Christian will never live a sinless life upon this earth, but with Jesus as the most important thing in life, sin will lose it's power to hold us down. Why is it that Jesus has this effect in the life of a Christian? It is because He came to live in this world, giving Himself as the perfect sacrifice that God demanded to attone for the sins that we have committed.

Jesus Christ is not only an example of how the Christian should live during this life; His life is what gives us the power to live as we are supposed to live. He has faced temptations of every kind and been victorious. He knows how to live victoriously in this life, and He loves us enough to guide us through this stormy existence.

Our verse tells us to consider Him that endured. This is why we should keep Him in front of us every minute, every day. When you wake up with the weight of the world on your shoulders, Satan knows he has a very easy target for the day. When you get discouraged with your job, your friends, your family, or just with life in general, the first thing you are going to want to do is forget about them, comfort yourself in some way, and follow the path of least resistance. When you see wicked people living it up and enjoying life, while you are struggling day after day, if you are not considering the One who gave up His life so that you can live, you are going to quit the Christian life.

It is during these times in life that the Christian must consider Jesus Christ. Consider the fact that He loved you so much that He left heaven and came to live as a man in this sinful world. Consider the fact that He walked among men who hated Him throughout His life, showing them nothing but love. Consider the fact that even as He was dying on the cross, He asked God to forgive them for what they had done to Him. Consider the fact that because you have sinned, you are one of those who put Him on the cross. Yet He loves you, and wants to see you have a successful Christian life today.

No other person who ever lived has had that kind of strength, focus, and love. No other person who ever lived has faced, and overcome, this kind of hatred and wickedness. No other person who has ever lived has been able to say that he is the perfect sacrifice for your sins and mine. No other person who has ever lived has ever cared about you as much as this man. He is waiting for you to consider Him. He is waiting for you to put your eyes upon Him, turn your worries and struggles over to Him, and let Him give you a victorious life.

When you feel as if you cannot go on any longer, consider what His love compelled Him to do for you.

Consider Christ when you're weary and worn
Consider Christ though by the world you've been torn
Consider Christ even though you may mourn
In His love for you He's been through all of this, and it's by His blood you've been reborn.

TURNING FAILURES INTO VICTORIES

Isaiah 40:28-31, "Hast thou not Known? Hast thou not heard, that the everlasting God, the LORD, the Creator of the ends of the earth, fainteth not, neither is weary? There is no searching of His understanding. He giveth power to the faint; and to them that have no might He increaseth strength. Even the youths shall faint and be weary, and the young men shall utterly fall: But they that wait upon the LORD shall renew their strength; they shall mount up with wings as eagles; they shall run, and not be weary; and they shall walk, and not faint."

As we walk this life, there is one thing increasingly obvious in the world around us: more and more people who were once excited about being Christians and living the Christian life are falling away; back into a sinful lifestyle, or just losing their excitement and giving up on the dreams they once had for God. I have seen many people "give their lives to Christ" one day, and the next day be discouraged to the point of quitting.

Many Christians have a very false understanding of what the Christian life is, and should be. They have been taught that being a Christian means God works for you and will give you a great life with fewer or no problems. While it is true that God will and does work on our behalf, the rest of that statement is the lie of Satan. He has conceived this deception to confuse, discourage, and defeat the Christian, and it works very well indeed.

No place in Scripture can we find God telling us that the Christian walk will be easy. Instead, we are promised a life filled with trials, temptations, and persecution. John 16:33, "These things I have spoken unto you, that in me ye might have peace. In the world ye shall have tribulation: but be of good cheer; I have overcome the world." James 1:2-4, "My brethren, count it all joy when ye fall into divers temptations; knowing this, that the trying of your faith worketh patience. But let patience have her perfect work, that ye may be perfect and entire, wanting nothing."

Through these trials and temptations that we face, we are promised victory, but only if we face them the right way. We often try to do things in our own power, following our own understanding, and it is then that have discouragement and failure. God has given us the power and strength to overcome the obstacles we face through faith in, and reliance upon Him. If we try it any other way, we will fail!

Each of us knows very well that we grow weary very easily. We can work all day, and at night, we must sleep and regain our strength to do it over tomorrow. The same is true in our spiritual walk. We must eat correctly, or we will not have the spiritual nourishment we need in our Christian walk. Even the little spiritual germs will hinder us. We must rest when it is time to rest, or we will not have the strength we need to get through the day. We are weak and frail, and we need the spiritual life-sustaining food and rest that only God can give. So often we forget how weak we are, and go off on our own. Life is so busy today; there is so much to be done, and so little time to get it all accomplished.

But we serve a God that NEVER gets weary. We serve a God that NEVER needs rest. We serve a God that understands everything we face in life, even if we understand nothing. We serve a God that can take our frail and weak lives and turn them into a powerhouse for His work! He wants to help us; to guide us; to love us; to provide for us.

The secret to the help He offers is in waiting. Our verses tell us that the youths shall be faint and weary, and that the young men shall utterly fall. We cannot do what He has put into our hearts to do! He has given us the desire, but we will never have the capability to do it. We must have His help; His power upon us to succeed. The word "wait" here does not mean to stop and do nothing; the picture here is one of a waitress "waiting" upon her customers. She finds out what they want, and provides for them. She is not just standing around to see if they will give her a tip; she is working for them. So must we be with God. Seek Him; follow Him; please Him; work on a relationship with Him; rest in Him; give Him our worries, and leave them with Him; let Him reward us by giving us victory in this life that we can never have on our own.

If we will approach Him like this, trying to please Him, He will give us the strength to walk and not faint, or give up in life. He will give us the ability to run the race set before us and not be hindered by weariness in the Christian life. He will turn our failures into victories, and our trials into blessings!

TURNING FEAR INTO FAITH

Isaiah 41: 9-10, "Thou whom I have taken from the ends of the earth, and called thee from the chief men thereof, and said unto thee, Thou art my servant; I have chosen thee, and not cast thee away. Fear thou not; for I am with thee: be not dismayed; for I am thy God: I will strengthen thee; yea, I will help thee; yea, I will uphold thee with the right hand of my righteousness."

There are many things to fear in life, and most of us are very good at taking advantage of these fears. There is danger in every aspect of our day; the drive to work; the dangers at the job; the list could go on and on for even the basic life of any person. Then when we turn the news on, we are made aware of a vast new dimension of fears from our enemies, as well as natural disasters that could happen anywhere, and at any given time.

If we allow fear into our lives, it will quickly consume us, and make us useless to God, our families, our friends, and anyone else who needs us. Satan uses fear to incapacitate us in life, and in spiritual things. Fear, if not checked very quickly, will take complete control of our lives, and will drive us from a lifestyle centered on pleasing and serving God back into our old lifestyle. This is Satan's goal for the Christian. He has already lost the war for our soul, but he is very good at wounding us and getting us out of the battle.

The Lord gives us some great promises in this passage. He tells us that He has taken us; He has called us to Him, and made us His servant. We know we cannot win this battle we face on a daily basis, but we also know that the God we serve is all powerful; He cannot lose, and our enemy cannot get anything around Him!

God has chosen us to be His servants. We can rest in the wonderful assertion that if we have been saved, we now belong to God; He will never cast us away! There are many religions out there that serve a god that can change his mind about his love for his servants. There is no guarantee at the end of life to be accepted by these gods. Many religions teach that one can lose the salvation their god has offered them if they stumble or fall. The God we serve understands that we are sinners, and that we cannot be perfect. The guarantee He gives is that if we turn to Him, He will NEVER cast us away.

We are told to fear not! Deuteronomy 31:6, "Be strong and of a good courage, fear not, nor be afraid of them; for the LORD thy God, Hi it is that doth go with thee; He will not fail thee, nor forsake thee." John 16:33, "These things I have spoken unto you, that in me ye might have peace. In the world ye shall have tribulation: but be of good cheer; I have overcome the world." There is no reason to fear any of the terrible things our enemy may cast into our path, for our God has overcome this world, and all the evil in it! He promises that He will be with us always, and that He will never leave us, or forget about us.

He goes on to tell us to "be not dismayed…" The meaning of this word is "to break down the courage of completely, as by sudden danger or trouble; dishearten thoroughly." There is only one way to do this: we must keep our eyes upon the object of our salvation: Jesus Christ. This world is a very hard and scary place to be. There are temptations and dangers on all sides, and only one way to overcome them! We can keep our courage to walk the path God wants us to walk if we keep our eyes on Him at all times. Satan will try to get us to look away; to be drawn away from the protection of our God, but if we remain with Him in faith, He will give us victory in life, even when it seems that there is no victory possible!

He further tells us in this passage that He will strengthen us. We simply cannot find the strength on our own to do what needs to be done, whether it is to take a stand for something we believe, or getting through temptations and trials. But if we remain focused on Him, He promises to give us the strength we need to do what needs to be done. He promises us help when we cannot do what we need to do. He promises to work on our behalf when we do not know what to do. He promises to work on, in, and through us to accomplish His will, and to walk the Christian life.

Lastly, He promises to "uphold thee with the right hand of my righteousness." We do not need to ever rely upon our own righteousness to please Him. In fact, Isaiah 64:6 tells us that we are all unclean; our righteousness is as filthy rags in His sight. The best that we can be is not even close to being acceptable to God. But if our trust in in Christ instead of ourselves, the righteousness God sees when He looks at us is not ours, but His own!

What we need can never be found in us; it can only be found in Jesus Christ. He provides the faith, the power, the righteousness, the security and the protection that we have spent our lives searching for, and He freely offers it to us. Our responsibility is to simply trust in Him. Trust in Him to bring us through the tests and trials of life, even when there is no way through them that we can see. If we will do this, we will see our fear and failures turn into faith and pure victory.

BECOMING NEW BY GIVING UP

2 Corinthians 5:17-18, "Therefore if any man be in Christ, he is a new creature: old things are passed away; behold, all things are become new. And all things are of God, who hath reconciled us to himself by Jesus Christ, and hath given to us the ministry of reconciliation;"

In our last passage, we talked about the faithfulness and power of God in forgiving us of our sins when we come to Him with true confession. This one tells us how we will begin to live after we have had this true confession. Confession, done right, is always accompanied by repentance. Repentance, often confused with being sorry for something, is actually a turning away from something. A person can be sorry he did something yesterday while at the same time doing it today. It accomplishes nothing but a remorseful life. Everyone knows someone who lives their entire life being sorry for their lifestyle, while doing nothing to change the way they live. Many of us, if we were to be honest about it, can tell of times we have done this very thing. It is pointless for a Christian to live this way!

Our passage tells us that if we are truly saved, we are a new creature. Before we came into a relationship with Jesus Christ, we had no other option than to live a remorseful life. We had no power to overcome the sin in our life. We were powerless to change our lives into something worth living. But, when we begin this walk with the Savior, Scripture tells us this has changed. Jesus has made us a new creation. While we will struggle with sin in our new life, there is one crucial difference in the old and the new person: the new person has the resources to change!

This passage goes so far as telling us that if we are saved, we have no choice but to be a new creation. The change that has taken place in the deepest part of our being is so powerful, it will make us despise the things we once did, the places we once went, the communication that once came out of our mouth, the things we once put into our body, the things we once looked at and took pleasure in. The list here can go on and on. What has replaced these desires we once had, and changed the things that once made us feel satisfied and happy is now a desire to live a life that glorifies God in all that we do. We no longer live for ourselves, but Jesus is living His life through us.

Verse 18 starts by telling us that "all things are of God, who hath reconciled us to Himself by Jesus Christ.." So often we fool ourselves into thinking that the change that has taken place in us has anything to do with us. This is where many become shipwrecked in the Christian life, and end up going back into their old lifestyle. If we believe the power to change has come from us, then we can begin to listen to ourselves for what is right or wrong. How often it is that a person who once had so much potential to have a great, God-pleasing life is dragged back deeper into a life of sin than he ever way before. But if we understand that this power to change has come not from us, but from God, we also realize that we must continue to listen to Him to let us know what is right and wrong, and to know how to live our lives.

All of these changes we have witnessed in our new life have come from God. All of the power over sin has come from God. Every victory we enjoy has come, not because of any power we possess, but from the God who has the best intentions for us. We must work to keep the communication lines strong with our Savior. Any relationship must be worked at to remain strong, and this one is no different. Are you enjoying new found freedom from a sin that once held you hostage? Go on and enjoy it by all means; but never forget where that freedom really came from. Take time today, and every day, to spend in communication with God. Listen to Him through His Word, and talk to Him through prayer.

Lastly, I would challenge you to examine your heart and life. Have you ever experienced this change in a true and lasting way? Do you truly know what it means to have a relationship with Jesus? If not, you can have it today. Put your faith in Jesus Christ, and see the true difference He will make in your life. You will never find true and lasting freedom, peace, and contentment, unless you find it in the One that created it. He can take a life that has been destroyed by sin and turn it into something more beautiful than you can ever imagine. It all begins by letting Him have the power in your life!

OASIS IN LIFE'S DESERT

Isaiah 43:19, "Behold, I will do a new thing; now it shall spring forth; shall ye not know it? I will even make a way in the wilderness, and rivers in the desert."

We Christians often get bogged down with the "old ways" of life. We find ourselves looking back on how things used to be, the things we used to do, the friends we used to have, and the paths that we used to walk. Many times we catch ourselves in a "rut," insisting on holding on to something that God wants us to let go of.

The reasons for this are many. We don't know any other way, and are scared of trying something and failing. We just like our lives the way they are, and don't want to give them up. Maybe it is a particular habit or sin we find ourselves constantly falling into, not even realizing what is happening until we wake up in the rut one day. Whatever the reason may be, we find that our joy and blessings stop coming in until we find a way to climb out of the rut we have dug ourselves into.

God is a God of new beginnings. Many times throughout Scripture we can read where He took a broken down person and made of him or her a complete, fulfilled person. This is why Jesus came to this earth. Our Lord loves to take our broken dreams, lives, and families into His arms and turn them into something beautiful and meaningful. The Christians part of this equation is to keep focused upon God. God wants to do marvelous things in the lives of each person alive today, but as always, it is the choice of the individual to allow or disallow God to work and build in his life.

We can often find that in our failures we have taken our focus off of God's desires, and put them on the things that we desire. The job we want, instead of the one that God had directed us towards. The house we want, in the town we want, instead of letting God plant us where He knows we would thrive and be useful to Him. Even those who are in service to Him often begin to have a change of heart; from knowing, loving, and having a great relationship with God, to helping others, having a ministry, or serving. God does want us to serve Him, but He is much more interested in something else.

1 Samuel 15:22, "And Samuel said, hath the LORD as great delight in burnt offerings and sacrifices, as in obeying the voice of the LORD? Behold, to obey is better than sacrifice, and to hearken than the fat of rams. For rebellion is as the sin of witchcraft, and stubbornness is as iniquity and idolatry." It is much more important in God's eyes that the Christian simply obey His leading in our lives. Even if the direction God gives, in our eyes, is going to cost much, or hinder our ability to serve, the thing most important to God is that you and I obey His voice, and His leading. We are not in charge of the outcome; our responsibility is obedience.

If we look at the way a plant grows, we understand that something had to die in order for the plant to be alive. A garden would never grow and produce fruit if the seeds that were planted refused to cooperate with the plans and intentions of the owner of the garden. But because the seed dies, a new plant is birthed, and much increase is given.

The same is true in the life of the Christian. You and I must be willing to let our dreams and goals die if we want to be used and blessed by God. Even in those instances when it seems we are giving up everything we have worked for. Even in those cases where our hard-earned work is destroyed. We have to choose to obey God, trusting that He has a goal in mind. We must allow Him to bring some things in our lives to an end, so that other things can have room to grow and thrive, planted there by the hand of God Himself.

Even if it seems that the new place He has brought us to has nothing for us. Can not the Creator of the universe put an oasis in the middle of a terrible desert land where existence is not possible? And it is only after that oasis is created that men can live there! In this new year, would you be willing to let God make an oasis of your life, where the thirsting souls of those who have no hope can have a drink of the living water?

God is the God of new. God is the God of life. But in order for you and I to have these things, we must be willing to die to our desires and goals. Make no mistake, these steps will hurt. It is never easy to let go of dreams and passions. But we must remember the fact that this very life we live is temporary. God wants us to live today for Him, and let Him worry about where we will be living tomorrow.

Matthew 6:33, "But seek ye first the kingdom of God, and His righteousness, and all these things will be added unto you." Will you purpose in your heart today to honor God, instead of men? Will you determine to please God in the next year, instead of yourself? The world will oppose this stand; they will fight hard against it. But if you will give your life this purpose, God will have honor and glory through your life, and many lives will be touched and changed for Him! Romans 8:31, "If God be for us, who can be against us?"

HOW TO HEAR FROM GOD

Isaiah 59:1-3, "Behold, the LORD'S hand is not shortened, that it cannot save; neither His ear heavy, that it cannot hear: "But your iniquities have separated between you and your God, and your sins have hid His face from you, that He will not hear. For your hands are defiled with blood, and your fingers with iniquity; your lips have spoken lies, your tongue hath muttered perverseness."

Many are the times in life that we find we cannot hear from God. Although this problem doesn't come overnight, it may seem to us that it happened just that way. One day we are living a good life, and the next day we are miserable and lonely. When we try to go to God for help, it seems as though our prayers barely get from our lips, and we know for certain that the Lord is not listening to us, or cannot hear us.

Many times this will make us doubt our salvation, or even His willingness to take care of us. We question His promises, His motives, His love, His ability, sometimes even His existence. The real problem is that we get stuck in verse one of this passage, thinking that somehow it is God's shortcomings or lack of concern for us. We wonder why He just won't come down and let us hear from Him.

When you find yourself in this condition, take a close look at verse two and three here. The problem is not with God; cannot be with God. God never moves. He is the same yesterday, today, and forever. His law is supreme, and if you break it, you have moved, and are guilty. It is you that breaks the relationship with Him, not the other way around. God cannot look at sin; He cannot ignore iniquity in your life.

Do you have unconfessed sin in your life? Are you ignoring His Word? If so, this is the reason that you cannot hear from Him. He is softly calling you to come to Him with a broken heart over your lawlessness. He longs for a wonderful relationship with you, but you must meet His standards. He longs to help you, but you must come with a heart that is willing to learn from Him; a heart that is willing to leave those things behind that hinder you from being in fellowship with Him.

God desires a relationship with you, but you must have your heart right with Him. While it is true that no person will ever live a sinless life, he can live a life that keeps confession of sin as a priority of life. If you allow the smallest sin to invade your life and refuse to deal with it, it will not only linger, but grow into bigger sin. The simplest way; the only way, to get rid of the sin in your life and be right with God is to confess to Him not only the sin in your life, but your inability to correct it. It takes Him. 1 John 1:9, "If we confess our sins, He is faithful and just to forgive us our sins, and to cleanse us from all unrighteousness." If we come to Him, on His terms, He will not only forgive us, He will make us clean. Then, once again, we will hear from God.

FULL AND HUNGRY

Philippians 4:11-13, "Not that I speak in respect of want: for I have learned, in whatsoever state I am, therewith to be content. I know both how to be abased, and I know how to abound: every where and in all things I am instructed both to be full and to be hungry, both to abound and to suffer need. I can do all things through Christ which strengtheneth me."

In these verses, we get to the full benefit of what having the God of peace with us in this life is. Paul tells us that he has learned to be content in whatever state he finds himself in. We know that Paul spent a lot of time in jail, unjustly. In his days before a relationship with Christ, we know him as a vile person, one who was ever trying to increase his power over other people, and even present at the murders of several saints. Now, to hear this statement come from him, we can be sure a huge change had come to him.

Just as Jesus Christ had this dramatic effect in the life of the Apostle Paul, if given a chance, He can and will do the same for us! There are undoubtedly many things in our lives that we want or need. So many Christians waste the best part of their lives away trying to get more, or better, things than they have already. But as we all know, even when we get those things that we so desire today, within just a little while, those things are no longer new to us, and we begin to want something else. Without the change in our lives that can only come from Jesus Christ, our lives will only ever be a roller coaster of ups and downs, seeking the newest and best things that life has to offer, stealing from us the joy, peace, and contentment that comes from seeking Christ first and foremost in life.

The secret to finding this place of contentment is found in verse eight. Thinking on the things in life that are true, honest, just, pure, lovely, of good report, virtue, and praise will allow Christ to transform us from creatures of vileness and unrest to ones that are perfectly content with whatever state we may find ourselves in, and will make us usable for the kingdom work that the Lord wants us to do.

Paul goes on to say that he knows how to be abased, or reduced in reputation, and how to abound, or to be lifted up. Paul was a Roman citizen, as well as a Pharisee. These two titles alone gave him much to be proud of, and respected for. If the change that Christ gave to him was one that could turn this kind of pride into the humility needed to keep loving even those that wanted to take his life, think of the power it could display in the lives of ordinary Americans going into work every day! This is what God wants you and I to have in this life; a changed life that everyone sees, so that God Himself is glorified through our daily lives.

Paul goes on to say that he is both full, and hungry; that he knows how to abound, and also how to suffer need. What he is saying is that he is full and content with the things God has given to him, as well as the troubles that God lets come his way, because he knows that God has a purpose in them all. He is perfectly at rest in the love and provision of God. Oh, that Christians today could find this place of contentment as we face the direction our country is going! At the same time that he is full and resting in God's provision, he is also hungry. He is hungry to see, hear, and know more from God. He is hungry to see God working in seemingly hopeless situations. He is hungry for a closer and more meaningful walk with his Savior. He is hungry to be used in greater ways, and for greater purposes than he has yet been used, no matter what these things might cost him physically. Paul found himself at a point in life that if the purpose of God could be fulfilled, even through his own death, he was perfectly willing for this to happen. Friends, this is the true meaning of being full, and hungry!

God has plans and desires for His children that we will never realize in our lives until we come to this place in our Christian walks. Are you ready for God to show you these beautiful ways He wants to use you in the lives of your friends and loved ones? Time is short; it will soon be too late to take those who are most important to us to our future home. We must do it today!

As impossible as this place is to find in our own power, God makes a way for us to find it. In verse 13, Paul tells the reader that it was never in his own power that he was able to find this peace and wonderful contentment, but it is through the power of Jesus Christ that this is found. Would you purpose in your heart today to rest completely in the love, mercy, and grace of the Lord, letting Him fill you with Himself, and empty you of worldly desires, so that He might live through you?

DECEPTION OR TRUE HEART KNOWLEDGE?

James 1:22-25, "But be ye doers of the Word, and not hearers only, deceiving your own selves. For if any be a hearer of the Word, and not a doer, he is like unto a man beholding his natural face in a glass: For he beholdeth himself, and goeth his way, and straightway forgetteth what manner of man he was. But whoso looketh into the perfect law of liberty, and continueth therein, he being not a forgetful hearer, but a doer of the work, this man shall be blessed in his deed."

Here we find another key element to living a life of victory and freedom. Many "Christians" want to have salvation, but think it is ok not to have a relationship with God. The problem with this is that it goes contrary to everything the Scripture teaches about true salvation.

In Mark Chapter 4, verses 3-8, we find Jesus telling a parable of a sower. We see that some seed that was sown fell by the way side and the birds ate it. Some seed fell on stony ground, and while it appeared at first to be growing, it had no nourishment, and soon died. Some of the seed fell among thorns, and yielded no fruit. Then we come to the seed that fell upon good ground. Jesus explained that this was the seed that actually grew, and then produced fruit. This is the only productive fruit that we find in this passage.

The seed that fell on stony ground can be related to our passage in James. Many people, even in the Church, are this seed. They have heard the Gospel message, and have even maybe said "The Sinners Prayer." The seed was planted, but they have never actually allowed the Word of God to make a difference in their lives. Upon a day that trouble or hardship comes, they will quickly fall away from the Christian lifestyle, because for some reason "it doesn't work for them."

The real trouble with these people is that they have heard the Word, but have not truly allowed Jesus Christ to make a difference in their lives. We could say they have a "head knowledge," but not a "heart knowledge." If we really want to be assured of a true salvation that will stand the test of time, it takes so much more than a prayer. This lifestyle requires a heart change; it requires good ground for the seed to grow; and if the seed grows in good ground, it will certainly reproduce itself.

What fruit can be found in the field of your heart and life? Our passage tells us with certainty that if we are hearers of the Word only, and not doers, that we have deceived ourselves. This is so much worse than being deceived by satan! If we have deceived ourselves, it simply means that we understand what is required of us, but we still want to do it our way. It means that we have come face to face with our true selves, realizing our faults and failures, and have just ignored the facts.

Then we see a picture of what it is to have looked into that mirror that Scripture provides, and seeing ones terrible reflection, have taken action upon it. This person is very aware that only Scripture can show a person their true self. Only Scripture can show one their faults. And only Scripture can provide the answer to one's terrible problem. This person continues in the perfect law of liberty; not because it holds him back, but because it gives him true freedom.

The restrictions found in the Scripture are not restrictions upon joy and happiness. Jesus said in John 10:10 that He has come that we might have life, and that we might have it more abundantly.

Don't allow the things this world calls fun to keep you from making a true commitment to Christ. Jesus Christ came to give us life to the fullest, but to receive this life requires more than a look into the Bible. It requires that we give the Bible a chance to have a look into us, and to make the changes needed.

DESTRUCTIVE DECISIONS

Proverbs 29:1, "He, that being often reproved hardeneth his neck, shall suddenly be destroyed, and that without remedy."

Recently, I drove through the campus of the Christian University where I began my college education. As I looked at the buildings where I sat in so many classes, in the buildings where I started so many friendships, and in the buildings where I worked and lived, it was a very sad moment for me. It was sad because these buildings that used to teach so many how to do the work of the Lord are now empty. The buildings where many lifelong friendships and even marriage relationships began now sit with shades drawn, and with no life whatsoever. As I drove through this campus, I was reminded of this verse, and it brought me to tears.

It is so very easy for the Christian to begin to allow unconfessed sin into his life. The longer he allows this to go on, the harder his heart becomes to the reproof of friends, family, and even the Holy Spirit. As sin in our lives is brought to our attention, no matter the source, we should make an immediate move to do whatever we have to do to remove this sin from our lives.

Satan will try to make us believe that our sin is just a little one; a sin that hurts no one. He will tell us that we can still be good Christians while we harbor this sin in our hearts. But God looks at things very differently. God gave His only Son so that you and I could have a chance for eternal life. That little sin we keep hidden away cost Jesus Christ His life! Make no mistake; it is the little sins that ruin lives, jobs, families, and even Churches.

1 John 5:16, "If any man see his brother sin a sin which is not unto death, he shall ask, and he shall give him life for them that sin not unto death. There is a sin unto death: I do not say that he shall pray for it." God strongly warns us about a sinful lifestyle. When we allow sin into our lives, the Holy Spirit will remind us that what we are doing is wrong. God will often even send friends and family to us to reprove us. If we refuse to correct what is wrong, we are opening the doors for serious consequences, maybe even death.

Today's society makes light of most sin. We watch it on TV, listen to it on the radio, pay to see it in public places, and ignore it when it is in our own lives. God does not make light of it at all. He warns us to live right, or face the consequences for our lack of doing so.

A sad, but true example of this is the campus I drove through. Once a lighthouse for God's Word and God's Work, they allowed many things to happen that God considered sin. As they continued to follow this path, it began to hurt the school, and even the Church that it belonged to. For many years, terrible decisions were made that did not honor God, and many leaders lived with sin in their private lives. God sent many to reprove them, but they would not hear it. Today, they no longer exist.

While the Christian may be able to hide his sin from the world and the Church, he will never succeed in hiding it from God. Don't make the mistake that many thousands of people have made throughout the history of this world. Deal with that sin that God is reminding you of today, while there is still a chance to do so.

"Sin will take you farther than you want to go, keep you longer than you want to stay, and cost you more than you want to pay."

YOUR TALENTS OR MINE?

Matthew 25: 14-30, "For the kingdom of heaven is as a man travelling into a far country, who called his own servants, and delivered unto them his goods. And unto one he gave five talents, to another two, and to another one; to every man according to his several ability; and straightway took his journey. Then he that had received the five talents went and traded with the same, and made them other five talents. And likewise he that had received two, he also gained other two. But he that had received one went and digged in the earth, and hid his lord's money. After a long time the lord of those servants cometh, and reckoneth with them. And so he that had received five talents came and brought other five talents, saying, Lord, thou deliveredst unto me five talents: behold, I have gained beside them five talents more. His lord said unto him, Well done, thou good and faithful servant: thou hast been faithful over a few things, I will make thee ruler over many things: enter thou into the joy of thy lord. He also that had received two talents came and said, Lord, thou deliveredst unto me two talents: behold, I have gained two other talents beside them. His lord said unto him, Well done, good and faithful servant: thou hast been faithful over a few things, I will make thee ruler over many things: enter thou into the joy of thy lord. Then he which had received the one talent came and said, Lord, I knew thee that thou art an hard man, reaping where thou hast not sown, and gathering where thou hast not strawed: and I was afraid, and went and hid thy talent in the earth: lo, there thou hast that is thine. His lord answered and said unto him, Thou wicked and slothful servant, thou knewest that I reap where I sowed not, and gather where I have not strawed: thou oughtest therefore to have put my money to the exchangers, and then at my coming I should have received mine own with usury. Take therefore that talent from him, and give it unto him which hath ten talents. For unto every one that hath shall be given, and he shall have abundance: but from him that hath not shall be taken away even that which he hath. And cast ye the unprofitable servant into outer darkness: there shall be weeping and gnashing of teeth."

The Lord often spoke in parables when He walked this earth. The stories He told then are even today very applicable to our lives, regardless of how much things have changed since Jesus walked this earth. We see here, first, that the master of these three men knew them well. He did not just hand out a bunch of money and hope for the best. He knew the strengths and weaknesses of each man, and knew what they were capable of doing, and made them responsible for what he knew they were able to be accountable for.

It doesn't take much effort today to find people with much more ability than many of us have; also, it doesn't take much effort to find those with less ability than we have. If we are not very careful in life, we will quickly find ourselves envying others for both their very important life and responsibilities, or their seemingly care free lifestyle of little or no responsibilities. When this happens, two things can be said of us, both equally true: We have made ourselves useless to our family and friends, and more important, we have made ourselves useless to the God who has given us gifts and talents that He want to see used for His glory and honor.

The Lord does not expect the same out of each person alive today. He has gifted each of us differently, and this for a purpose. There are many jobs that must be done in order for the church as a whole to do what it is called to do. If even one of these jobs is left undone, it makes the church lopsided and inefficient. This is why our enemy has led us to believe the grass is always greener on the other side. If he can get you or I to quit doing the job God has for us, he has hindered the work of the Church without ever having to do battle with the leaders of the Church. If he can get to a person and make them think their job is unimportant, and discourage them to the point of giving up, just because they are not a "leader" in something, he has hobbled the entire ministry. We must understand that just because we may not have a visible role in the workings of things, each one of us is important to the whole! Just because you may not be gifted and talented in some areas will never mean that you are not needed, nor does it mean that you are any less important to the Lord than that person who has many talents.

Because God has designed each one of us with different abilities, He also knows how much we can accomplish with those abilities. He will never ask more from you than He made you capable of producing. If you are one of those with many different talents, He also will never overlook the way you may misuse what He has given you. At "the end of the day," we will each stand before our heavenly Father and give account of the way we have used what He has gifted us with. We will not be judged for the amount we have done compared with others; how could a just God expect as much from one holding one talent as He does from one holding five? We will be judged on the quality of the work which we have done.

Next, we see in this passage the man who was given only one talent. This man didn't have the ability of the other two, and the master knew it. He did, however, have the ability to be useful, as we can see in the fact that his master gave him anything at all. The problem in this man's life was not that he was not given enough to do something profitable for his lord; the problem was in his perception of his lord.

This man was brought to answer for what he had done, and started out by telling his master that he was a hard man, that he reaped things he had not sown, and gathered where he had not put forth any labor. He finished by telling his lord that he was afraid, and hid what he had been given to make a profit with. This man had the perception that his ruler was a hard person to get along with; that he took what shouldn't be his, and that he profited by other peoples labor. He had a terrible attitude towards the very person who had given him what he needed to succeed in life; and even to be an exceptional person.

So many times when we look at those with more abilities than us, we begin to harbor bitterness towards the very One who wants us to be a success in life. The more we look at others, the more bitter we get, and soon that bitterness will become a form of hatred and belligerence toward the God who loves us. We let the enemy fill us with lies about He who loves us more than anything. Instead of seeing a God of love, and a God who will provide for our lives and give us the ability to be a successful Christian, we begin to see an unjust God who demands things that we cannot do.

We have all heard the saying, "Attitude is everything," and in this case especially, it is very true. We have a choice today to look to our Father in heaven and either thank Him for the gifts He has given, and ask for His help and wisdom to make something out of them, no matter what or how many we have, or to look towards Him with an accusing attitude, telling Him that He is unjust to have not given us as much as others in our life, and to refuse to use what we do have for His glory and honor. We need to remember another old saying, "There's a payday, someday." We will each stand before a just and righteous God one day to give account of not the many talents of others, but the few that were left in our hands to employ for God.

GIVE, OR IT MAY BE TAKEN AWAY

Genesis 22:2, "And He said, take now thy son, thine only son Isaac, whom thou lovest, and get thee into the land of Moriah; and offer him there for a burnt offering upon one of the mountains which I will tell thee of."

Abraham is known as the father of many nations. God named him this many years before the verse we just read. God had promised Abraham that he would be the patriarch of a great nation, and that the entire world would be blessed by this nation. After this promise was given to him, Abraham spent many childless years, wondering how and when this promise would be fulfilled, because his wife could not have children. At the age of 100, Abraham saw the beginning of the fulfillment of this promise with Isaac being born. It was a blessed memory; a joyous occasion for Abraham and his wife, Sarah. It was also a great proof of the faithfulness of God to fulfill His promises.

Many years later, God is telling Abraham, in this verse, to take his son Isaac and offer him for a burnt offering to God. It was without a doubt a very hard command for Abraham to hear from the God he served with all his heart, and one that would be easy to ignore. We can gain much insight on what God wants from us through understanding this story.

Isaac was the fulfillment of a promise; one through whom the complete promise would come to pass. Abraham knew this would not happen in his lifetime, and he knew that Isaac and his seed would have the favor of God. And as an only child, his parents no doubt took much pleasure in providing him with much favor of their own. It is therefore easy for us to understand how this boy would mean so very much to his parents.

Perhaps the reason for the command that God had given in this verse can also be seen in the heart of this story. Isaac, being the promise of God to Abraham, had probably taken the most important role in the heart of this great man of the faith. Sure, he was thankful to God for this "child of his old age," and wanted the best for him, but it is quite possible that Isaac had become more important and more real to Abraham than the God he served. Before Isaac, Abraham had spent much time in prayer and communion with God, but after the promise arrived, much of the time previously spent with God became taken up by the thing he had prayed so fervently for.

Abraham, when this command was given him, knew the true meaning of making the choice to follow God, or making the decision to reject Him altogether. He understood exactly what was required of him to remain in communion with God; the sacrifice of his beloved son. He knew the consequences to himself of rejecting God's command; he also knew the consequences to his loved ones if he obeyed it. How could a God that professed to love him so much ask so very much of him? How could he obey this command and ever hope to see the fulfillment of the promise that was made so many years ago? All of these questions were going through his mind as he made the three day journey to the mountain the sacrifice would be made upon.

In verses 9-10 of this chapter, we see Abraham bind his own son and put him on the altar. In verse 12, God said, "Lay not thine hand upon the lad, neither do thou anything unto him; for now

I know that thou fearest God, seeing thou hast not withheld thy son, thine only son from me." As Abraham was seconds away from ending the life of his son, God stopped him from doing so. Abraham had just passed the ultimate test of faith. Without doubt, he had many questions as to what God was doing, but he was determined to obey no matter the cost. Abraham could have tried to ignore this command, or explain it away, to protect his son, but we can see today how God has blessed so greatly, because Abraham would hold nothing back from Him.

The question for today, is, what is YOUR Isaac? As you look at your life, what has become bigger than God to you? Maybe it is a dream that God Himself has given you, and like Abraham, this dream has gotten between your heavenly Father and you. Maybe it is a job, or a spouse. Maybe it is a ministry that God has called you to, and given you a drive to reach people with His love and His formula for living a free and happy life. No matter what it is, no matter how good it is, even if it is something that God has promised you or put on your heart to do, once it becomes bigger and more important than your relationship with God, it becomes wrong.

If God sees something in your life that is hindering you from having a growing relationship with Him, one of two things will happen with it. 1: He wants you to understand what you are doing wrong, and He wants you to willingly put it in its rightful place, behind Him, or 2: He will remove it from your life.

He will try to warn you; wake you up to what you are allowing to happen, and give you a chance to correct it yourself, just as He did with Abraham. But if it is something you are trying to hold back from Him, you had better be prepared to lose it altogether. We serve a God that loves us dearly; too much to allow us to put something in His place. We serve a God with much power to give; but also much power to take away.

What is it that He is asking you to give up to Him? What thing is so important that you would try to shield it from God? What He is asking you to do could only be a test to see how much you love Him. If you give it up to Him, you may not really lose it at all, as in Abraham's case. But if you are not willing to give it to God, God may very well take it from your life for good.

ALTAR OF THE HEART

Genesis 35:2-3, "Then Jacob said unto his household, and to all that were with him, put away the strange gods that are among you, and be clean, and change your garments; and let us arise, and go up to Bethel; and I will make there an altar unto God, who answered me in the day of my distress, and was with me in the way which I went."

Throughout the earlier part of his life, Jacob was, we know from Scripture, a liar and a conniver, doing anything he needed to do to get what he wanted. His name means "supplanter." In his early years, nothing was sacred to him. He undoubtedly knew that God had chosen him, instead of his brother, Esau, from which to bring forth the nation that would bless the world with the Messiah. But even knowing that God would bless and use him greatly, Jacob struggled in a big way with sin in his life. We see this verse as Jacob was getting ready to flee from where he had been living, fearing that the people of the land would kill his entire family.

Jacob had seen God step in time after time throughout his life, offering to fix his problems and bless him. Time after time, Jacob had taken the blessings from God and used them up on his own agenda. But this time, Jacob started getting it right. He knew that most of the problems and struggles he had was a result of not following God with his whole heart. He was just starting to see the consequences to his family of his lifestyle of halfhearted service and surrender to God.

Many are the times that the Christian finds himself in the same condition today. God allows things to happen to bring us back to Him, because He loves us dearly. We can see here the steps we need to take when we find ourselves off course and out of the blessings of God. God does want to bless us and provide for us, but He will not bless our sinful lifestyles, and He cannot bless us if we are following other gods.

We can only start this process by examining our hearts to find the strange gods that we have put over the one true God. Jacob knew what his gods were, and was determined to banish them from his life. He also knew that he could never find the gods that his family was following. This is a personal decision, and cannot be done by anyone other than the individual. These gods can be anything; people, jobs, cars, property—the list goes on and on. The false god in your life and mine is anything that takes precedence over the Lord God. Until you and I are ready to give up these gods, we will never be able to truly worship and serve the real God. He will not coexist with another god!

Next, Jacob told his family to be clean. When we walk in this world, chasing its gods, we become dirty, inside and out. The purification process is not always a simple one. I make a living installing industrial tires, and at the end of the day, I am usually very nasty. If I take a simple bar of soap and wash by quickly rubbing it over my hands and arms, I will be just as dirty when I get done as I was before I started; I have wasted my time! The cleaning process after a day at my job is to use abrasive soap and a brush, and scrub hard. This scrubbing often times hurts, but it is necessary if I want to get clean.

On a spiritual level, the Word of God is the abrasive soap that we must use. We must get it into our hearts by studying it, meditating on it, and applying it to our lives. It will show us things about ourselves that we didn't know were wrong, or that we have been hiding from ourselves. It will often hurt to clean these things out of our lives, but if we want to walk with God, we cannot skip this part. God will not live in a dirty house.

Then we must make a move. God wants His children to live in a different place than the world lives. When the Lord saved you, He didn't save you so you can continue to live a life of sin. Though He saved us while were in sin, He commands us to live a life worthy of His name. We cannot continue to live as we did before Christ came into our lives. He expects us to change where we go, what we look at, what we talk about, and the people we allow to influence our lives.

Finally, it requires an altar. God has brought us a new life in a dead world. God allows us to live around spiritually dead people, so that they might have a chance at the same new life He has given us. This altar should be our very lives. We are left here so that we might point others to Christ. Every aspect of the Christians life should point to, and praise and glorify God.

Jacob got tired of running from God, and placing other things in front of God in his life. As he studied his life, he realized that the problems he was facing were his own fault, and he determined that he would rid his heart from the things that caused him to keep stumbling and falling. He decided to follow God with his whole heart.

What is it today that is keeping you from the blessings of God? What is it that is keeping you from following God with your whole heart? Are you willing to go through the painful purification process so that God can make your life a thing of beauty?

GOD MEANT IT UNTO GOOD

Genesis 50:20, "But as for you, ye thought evil against me; but God meant it unto good, to bring to pass, as it is this day, to save much people alive."

There is not a person reading this who has not been a victim of evil doing. We have each been on the receiving end of terrible things done for the perceived benefit of the one who has done us wrong. Many times when this happens to us we can have a tendency to want to strike back against the person who has done us wrong. We have talked about how we can Biblically handle these feelings here in the past. Today, I would like to address another problem that goes along with these feelings.

Another huge problem mistreatment makes for the victim is that it creates an inability to trust people again. If you have been hurt by a good friend, you naturally have a defense mechanism that goes up, putting up a mental wall that makes it impossible for others to get close enough to you to be "that friend" again. This happens without you putting any thought into it. But as time goes on, without you taking aggressive action against it, you begin to see this wall in yourself, and you begin to see the fact that you are shutting others out.

The story of Joseph's life is one of the best stories we can study in times like this. He had been made fun of by his own family, and then sold by his own brothers into slavery. After being brought into Potifer's house, and being a faithful servant to him, he was again betrayed, and lied about by Potifer's wife. Just when it looked like things were beginning to get better for Joseph, he found himself in prison. While in prison, he again saw some hope of survival, when he interpreted dreams for Pharaoh's baker and cup bearer, only to be forgotten at the time he most needed to be remembered.

Very few people have had as much to complain about as Joseph. He spent many terrible years, accused of things he had never done, hated by his own family, and forgotten by his friends. In all of this time, Joseph kept his eyes on the one thing that mattered more than any other: his relationship with the Lord. Without question, there were many times in his life that he questioned what God was doing in his life. Without doubt, he spent many sleepless nights, with tears as his only companion. Yet, he never turned away from the Lord.

He also never allowed the wall we mentioned a minute ago to go up in his life. He knew that he was serving God, and he knew the truth about the false accusations that had developed into these terrible circumstances. He had every reason to refuse to trust anyone. He had every reason to refuse to open himself up to anyone. But he knew that God was at work, even though he didn't know if he would ever see justice done to his enemies.

Friend, if we allow the walls in our lives to go up after being hurt, God will never be able to use us in His work. If we refuse to open our hearts to people because we are afraid of being hurt again, the rest of our lives will be over spiritually. It is never fun when these things happen to us, but we must understand that if we are trying to live for the Lord, we have a powerful enemy, and they will happen to us.

Sometimes, God will allow these terrible things to happen to us because He is trying to build us into the person He wants us to be. Sometimes God has to move us out of our comfort zone to be able to use us. If we shut down when things get hard, we will be useless to God. We must keep our eyes focused upon God. We must keep serving Him, wherever we may end up in life. We must be willing to open our hearts to others, even after we have been hurt, and at the risk of being hurt again. We must remember that God knows the truth, and those who do wrong will be judged by Him, at some point; not only this, but the fact that God has allowed it to happen to us for a purpose.

If we will keep our eyes focused upon God, instead of the wrongdoings of others, and be willing to follow Him wherever the path leads, we will be able to say, as Joseph did, "But as for you, ye thought evil against me; but God meant it unto good, to bring to pass, as it is this day, to save much people alive."

Don't let the enemy have the victory in your life because of the lies or hurts of others. Stay focused on the One who matters. Stay available to Him, wherever you are in life. Take your struggles and heartaches to Him, and allow Him to keep molding you, through the pain you suffer. You will never know what God is going to bring your way while you are in the prison, but you can be sure that God knows you are there, and that He has placed you there for a specific purpose. No one loves you as the Lord does, and no one other than Him has the ability turn a nightmare into a wonderful, victorious dream.

TO COMPREHEND THE LIGHT

John 1:3-5, "All things were made by Him; and without Him was not anything made that was made. In Him was life; and the life was the light of men. And the light shineth in darkness; and the darkness comprehended it not."

These verses tell us, first, that everything we see and know about was created by the Almighty, Creator God. You and I are here today, not because of our mom and dad, but because God created us. The miracle of how a new born baby comes into this world is something that science cannot explain to this day. We know about the process, but we cannot explain how it possibly works. Throughout the Old Testament, we can read of many couples that tried for years to have a child, but were not able to have one until God's timing was right for them to conceive. Life was created in the beginning, by God, and to this day, life is still created, and given, by God Almighty.

"In Him was life; and the life was the light of men." Since life is given by God, it is only reasonable to conclude that it is God that can tell us the way to have a life that is fulfilled and peaceful. It is God that mankind must look to for direction and understanding. It is only God that can bring the fulfillment and peace that we each long for in life. The things that we become addicted and enslaved to are things that we originally went to, looking for them to fill the emptiness we have in our lives without God. This verse tells us clearly that in God is life, and His life is the light of men. If we refuse to allow God into our lives, we will live our lives in darkness. This is true for the unsaved person, but also for the saved person who has turned from God, back to the sins of his past.

The next verse tells us that the light shined into the darkness, but the darkness didn't comprehend it. It is this verse that we need to understand, if we want to understand what is happening in the world today, and also if we want to have the peace and contentment that is promised to the Christian in Scripture.

Mankind has lived in darkness since the first moment that Adam and Eve sinned in the Garden of Eden. Before they sinned, they had a relationship with God, but after they sinned, they were unable to walk with Him. Each of us also has sin; we have willingly turned away from God, His love, and His rules. When Christ came to live upon this earth, He came to shine the light into this dark world. He wanted to restore what mankind had thrown away.

The word "comprehend" means to "take hold of something," or to understand it. Another meaning of the word is to overpower something. The world cannot understand who Christ is, or what He desires for it, and so it fights against it. Many religions try to obey the Law, thinking that God gave the Law so that men might be redeemed. In truth, there is not one person who can keep this Law. God gave the Law so that mankind might understand how hopeless we are. There is no way possible for us to attain the lifestyle of sinless perfection that is required by God for admittance into His presence.

Some others think that they will be okay as long as they truly believe what they believe, or if they just do the best they can in life. But if we only sinned once in our entire lives, that one sin would be enough to keep us from the presence of God, because the Law He has given demands perfectness. In truth, Jesus was, and is, the light of the world. It is by Him, and through Him, that life was given, and it is only by Him, and through Him, that life can be sustained.

Our flesh, along with the world, is constantly fighting against God, and His desires for us. We want what will make us feel good right now, but God wants what is best for us in the long run. We want what will benefit us right now, but God wants what will benefit us is eternity. Our flesh cannot comprehend His plan for us, and will fight against it until the day we die. But because of His love for us, Jesus has given us the light of the Word of God, and the Holy Spirit to dwell inside us.

Through His Word, we can be changed from the inside. Because of His Spirit dwelling inside us, we can have the power to overcome the flesh that fights against Him constantly. Many Christians go up and down the roller coaster of life, wondering why they keep falling back into the same sins they battle with every day. Why can they not achieve the victory that is promised them in Scripture? The simple answer to this question is, because they do not allow the Spirit to guide and control them, and because they do not give the Lord the time required in His Word to change them.

Darkness is simply the absence of light. There are no levels of darkness, and there is no way to measure it. Light, on the other hand, can be measured. We can measure great distances in space by the speed that light travels. We can have more light, or less light in a room, by turning on, or off, some lights. The one thing you will never find in a brightly lit room is darkness. Darkness can only be defeated by light. The brighter the light, and the closer we are to the light, the less darkness will be found around us.

Are you finding yourself losing more battles with the sins you struggle with than the battles you win? Do you wish you had the peace and contentment that the Word of God promises? Do you want victory over the strongholds in your life that just won't let go? If so, the answer is to stop fighting the light, and to begin to draw closer to it. As you spend more time with the source of light, the darkness in your life will begin to be pushed out by His light.

THE LIGHT THAT GIVES DARKNESS

Luke 11:33-36, "No man, when he hath lighted a candle, putteth it in a secret place, neither under a bushel, but on a candlestick, that they which come in may see the light. The light of the body is the eye: therefore when thine eye is single, thy whole body also is full of light; but when thine eye is evil, thy body also is full of darkness. Take heed therefore that the light which is in thee be not darkness. If thy whole body therefore be full of light, having no part dark, the whole shall be full of light, as when the bright shining of a candle doth give thee light."

In these verses, Jesus is talking about something that probably every one of us take for granted: light. When we come into a dark room, we cannot see where we are going, or what we are doing, so we reach out and turn on a light, so we can see. To us, it is a simple flick of a switch, and beautiful, bright light illuminates the room we wish to see into. Few of us would turn a light on, just to turn our backs and walk away from the room we just illuminated. None of us would try to work, or accomplish a task in a room, or a workshop, without first making sure we had adequate lighting to accomplish our goals.

In the days of Jesus, it was much harder to achieve good lighting to give light to work, or see by. Even to start a flame was often a huge undertaking. A flint and steel were not much good when the wind was blowing; and even a small draft could extinguish the flame on a candle that was vital to see by. Even after lighting a candle, there was barely enough light given by the single flame to work by.

Jesus is saying, in verse 33, that no one would go through the work of creating a light, simply to put it in a place where it serves no purpose for anyone to see anything by it. No one would put this candle in a closet, or under a bush. Instead, after spending time to light the candle, a person would put it in a high place, in the middle of the room, where it would give light for all who were in the room to see and work by.

On a spiritual level, it is just the same. Jesus has created a way for us to have a restored relationship with the Father. He has gone through intense labors to provide this way for us. He took upon Himself the body of a human, leaving His glory and majesty behind, only to come and live a life as a hated individual, and to be murdered, and placed upon a hill, for all to see. He did this because He loved us, and because this was the only way possible for us to have this restored relationship with God.

Because He has given you and I this precious salvation, He expects something from us. We have been given the responsibility of holding the light up so those around us can see by it. The world lives in darkness, and they have no way of turning on a light. Jesus has placed the only source of light for this world within us, by giving the Holy Spirit to dwell with us. The warning here is to keep our eyes upon Jesus Christ. As we look at Him, and spend time with Him, His light will permeate us, and we will become walking candlesticks, shining the light every place we go. But if we turn our focus upon other things in this world, the light coming from within us begins to grow dim; we have begun to hide our candle in a secret place.

Jesus cautions us against letting our light grow dim. Not only is it very dangerous for the Christian to begin to turn his focus from Jesus, to other things, but it is catastrophic to the world around us. As Christians, we have this light within us. We cannot lose the light; it will guide us into eternal life in the presence of God. But the world around us has no source to find this precious light aside from the Christian being willing to share with them. "Take heed therefore that the light which is in thee be not darkness."

Recently, I was with one on my sons at a local restaurant, when an older gentleman walked in, wearing a leather jacket with the word, NAVY on it. My son went over to the man, and told him that we would like to buy his supper in appreciation for his service to our country. It made the man's night, and he told us that this had never happened to him before. As my son and I finished our supper, it occurred to me that I should ask the gentleman about his relationship with the Lord. I felt in my pocket for the Bible that I sometimes carry, and it was not there. I checked to see if I had any gospel tracks, and did not. I told myself that I couldn't talk to the man with nothing to give him, or to show him, and so I decided that I would have to let this opportunity pass. This decision has haunted me since we drove out of the parking lot of the restaurant.

As a Christian, I failed that night. I will have to answer to God for the excuse I used for not talking to this man about a God who loves him, and wants him to spend eternity in Paradise. But even worse, if that man is not a Christian, I will have to answer to God for refusing to share the light that was given to me freely. And worse yet, if this man dies as an unbeliever, he will forever be punished for my lack of love towards him.

Friends, we have a huge responsibility upon our shoulders. We are the light holders. If we hide our light, the world around us will pay for our mistakes for eternity. Matthew 6:23, "…If therefore the light that is in thee be darkness, how great is that darkness!" Would you commit, with me, to make it a point of your life to hold up your candle? Time is running out quickly, and those who die without seeing the light we hold will spend eternity in complete and utter darkness.

HIS PEACE FOR YOUR BURDENS

Matthew 11:28-30, "Come unto me, all ye that labour and are heavy laden, and I will give you rest. Take my yoke upon you, and learn of me; for I am meek and lowly in heart: and ye shall find rest unto your souls. For my yoke is easy, and my burden is light."

Countless people go through life trying to make themselves good enough to have a hope of heaven upon the death of their bodies. They know that God is perfect, and that He requires the same of anyone who would have a relationship with Him. They read the Bible, seeing the Law that God has given, and struggle to be good enough. Some think that if they work hard enough, God just might dismiss their sinfulness, and allow them admittance into His presence.

Many others understand that they can never attain this salvation for themselves, and that it is given by the grace and mercy of God, but after receiving this gift of God, they fear that salvation can be lost by one way or another. Because of this, they spend their lives in fear of not being good enough for God when they reach the end of their lives. They believe that although salvation was given to them, they must work to retain God's love and favor.

Friend, if one of these descriptions is true of you, God wants you to know that they are both lies of Satan. Your enemy would have you believe that you must work for the gift of salvation from God, but God says He loves you enough to take you just the way you are. Your enemy would have you believe that you can lose what God has freely given, but God says that you cannot lose what His Son has purchased and given to you.

Jesus knows what each one of us knows very well: there is nothing that we can do to live up to His requirements. This is the very reason He came to this earth to give His own life so that we might have life. What He wants us to understand is the fact that He wants us to quit trying to be good enough for Him. He tells all of those who are working for His favor to just come to Him in faith. He has done the work required for our eternal life.

If we would just be willing to put our faith in what He has done, instead of trying to live up to something we could never attain, He tells us that we will find true rest. Instead of working or hoping, Jesus tells us that if we would just come to Him in faith, He would give us what we are seeking.

Next, He tells us that instead of trying to be good enough, trying to follow the path to a legalistic salvation that doesn't exist, we should just trust Him to be good enough. The path that mankind tries to take to God is filled with rules that no person can keep. As we make changes to ourselves, we find that these changes never stick anyway. We constantly fight the same struggles, when we are fighting in our own strength. The yoke of man-made laws and traditions is much too heavy a load for us to try to carry.

The yoke that Jesus will put upon us is one that He will help us pull. Self righteousness always holds up the self-righteous person, only to push those around him down. The yoke of Jesus is one that will display humbleness and meekness to the world around us; one that will draw others to follow.

Lastly, the message in these verses is for the one who is carrying burdens to great to bear. This life is hard, physically, emotionally, and spiritually. We see this every day, as we struggle to live a life that is pleasing to God. We have a very powerful enemy, who is constantly seeking a way to destroy us. The ways he uses are ruthless. He turns family and friends against us, and makes our lives unbearable in any way possible. Jesus is telling us in these verses that He, and He alone, can help us find our way through these obstacles that Satan is putting up for us.

Have you been trying to find your own way to victory in this life? Have you been working to make yourself good enough to come to God? Are you trying to carry the cumbersome burdens that you have picked up in this life, all by yourself? If so, the Lord is asking you to just come to Him, and let Him help you. He offers to take your unworthiness and replace it with His righteousness. He offers to give you a salvation that you cannot lose, because He has purchased it with His blood. He offers to take the burdens that are crushing you, and replace them with peace and contentment, knowing that He has it all under control. Are you willing to stop trying, and start believing?

A DIRTY CUP

Matthew 23:25-28, "Woe unto you, scribes and Pharisees, hypocrites! For ye make clean the outside of the cup and of the platter, but within they are full of extortion and excess. Thou blind Pharisee, cleanse first that which is within the cup and platter, that the outside of them may be clean also. Woe unto you, scribes and Pharisees, hypocrites! For ye are like unto whited sepulchers, which indeed appear beautiful outward, but are within full of dead men's bones, and of all uncleanness. Even so ye also outwardly appear righteous unto men, but within ye are full of hypocrisy and iniquity."

In these verses, we see Jesus warning against hypocrisy in our lives. Verse 25 begins by talking about cleaning the outside of a cup, but leaving the inside filthy and germ infested while drinking from it. Not one of us would do something so fool hearty to our physical bodies. We would never allow ourselves, or our loved ones, to drink from a glass that had been full of sewer water just moments ago, but poured out and simply wiped off. That glass, while it may appear pretty, would be full of invisible germs that are toxic for the body. But so often, this is exactly what we do spiritually. Though our lives are filled with secret sins and bondage, we find ourselves more concerned with what we look like to the world than with what we look like to the Lord.

Jesus goes on to talk about hypocrisy being like making the outside of a tomb pretty, and putting fresh paint on it. There are many cemeteries that we can look at which are beautiful. The grass is kept neat, the trees are trimmed nicely, and everything looks very nice. But we all know the truth of the matter is that these places are filled with the dead, decaying, rotting bodies of people who no longer have any appreciation or need for the beautiful scenery.

The point Jesus is trying to make here is that appearing clean on the outside is of absolutely no benefit to us, the people around us, or to God Himself. While we may fool others for a while, if we try to live this way, the truth will come out at some point. Many people, such as the Pharisees of Jesus' time, even fooled themselves into thinking they were OK because they outwardly obeyed the laws, and the traditions of men.

There are many today who believe that they can please God by doing good works, or outwardly practicing religion. They try to show the world how good they are by being a "good Christian" when they are in public, while their private lives are in chaos because of sin. But Scripture tells us in 1 Samuel 16:7, that God looks upon our hearts to see who we really are. God looks upon us from the inside, and this is what He is concerned about. If we follow the rules of religion outwardly, but inwardly have no love for Him, He says our very lives are like the whited sepulchers that Jesus was talking about; while they may be pretty and put together nicely on the outside, they have absolutely nothing of value on the inside, and actually do more to harm the health of those around us than we will ever do for good.

Why do we so often spend all of our time concerned with our outward appearance, and so little time with our inward cleanliness? We would be much better off by letting God show us what

He is dissatisfied with in our lives, and letting Him change these things. God will never be able to bless and use us for His purpose until we allow Him to clean us from the inside, out. If we are trying to tell others about Him while there is no evidence of Him in our personal lives, the only thing we will do is push them away from the God who loves, and wants to change them.

While God is interested in what the outside of our lives looks like, He is much more interested in what our heart looks like. A clean heart is not something that we can make by practicing religion, or by trying to hide our sins from God and the world. This can only be a work of the Lord in our lives, and until we give Him full access to the desires, and problems of our hearts, the best we can do is clean the outside, while leaving the filth of sin and self-righteousness on the inside. King David said, in Psalm 119, that God's Word is a lamp, and a light. Will you allow God to use the Scripture to clean the inside, so He can use the outside?

THE SECRET TO GETTING WHAT YOU WANT

James 4:1-4, "From whence come wars and fightings among you? Come they not hence, even of your lusts that war in your members? Ye lust, and have not: ye kill, and desire to have, and cannot obtain: ye fight and war, yet ye have not, because ye ask not. Ye ask, and receive not, because ye ask amiss, that ye may consume it upon your lusts. Ye adulterers and adulteresses, know ye not that the friendship of the world is enmity with God? Whosoever therefore will be a friend of the world is the enemy of God."

Have you ever wondered why we have so much war and unrest in the world? Have you ever wondered why people can't just be happy with what they have, or work hard to earn what they want? The answer is right here in this passage.

We have so many desires in life, and many of them conflict with one another. For instance; most of us want to live in a nice house, drive a nice car, and have a good job with a happy family. On the other hand, many of us have spent years chasing the best party, the best and most expensive time out on the town, etc. When we really sit down to study why it is that we have no money, we find that we have blown it all on foolishness.

We want that happy family, but spend all our time with our single friends, looking at, and longing for the old way of life when we had only ourselves to worry about. Or maybe it's the job we have that is keeping us away constantly. We cannot have what we want, simply because we hinder it ourselves!

The same is true spiritually. You may want to have a great relationship with God, but just can't understand why that will not happen. Study the problem out. Do you spend time with Him on a daily basis? Do you go to Church every time the doors are open? Are you showing Him with your prayer life and your actions that you want to know Him? Nothing in the spiritual life happens by chance! It takes commitment. There will be many challenges along the way. You will be faced with those temptations that your enemy knows will be absolutely hardest for you to overcome. It is one thing to dream of something, but something entirely different to make a goal of your dreams! Once we have a goal in life that we are focused on and committed to, our actions will show it.

Another reason in this passage is simply because we don't ask God for it. We try to do things in our own power, our own way, and on our own time frame. There may be something you desire that God really wants you to have, and He would be more than willing to give it if we would only ask Him.

Finally, each person should seek his/her true motivations for wanting something. If you have truly made something a goal, and are willing to work hard for it, and are asking God for it; why do you want it? This passage tells us that many that do ask God for something are only asking Him; here we go again, because of our own lusts. Sometimes Christians want a "position" in the Church because of the power and prestige it will give them. Many times people want other people to see them, for the simple sake of being talked about. What a terribly selfish and wasteful goal!

Our true motivation in everything we do should come from our love for Jesus Christ, who gave Himself a ransom for us! It is only because He loves us so very much that we have any hope, and yet we so often take it for granted, blowing our life on fruitless goals.

The only way we will ever be able to live above our lusts and sinful desires is by living for Christ! In fact, the only way we will ever be able to live in true peace with God is by living for Christ in all, and with all, that we do. We cannot hope to have His blessing upon our lives, and His help with our problems, while we still have our focus and desires upon this world and its pleasures.

Let's commit today to take our eyes off the world around us, and our affections from worldly goods, and put them upon the One who was willing to pay for a worthless sinner with His very own priceless blood; not out of His own lusts, but for our perfection!

WILL YOU BE HEALED?

John 5:5-6, "And a certain man was there, which had an infirmity thirty and eight years. When Jesus saw him lie, and knew that he had been now a long time in that case, He saith unto him, Wilt thou be made whole?"

This story takes place at the pool of Bethesda, a pool where many miracles of healing had taken place. The Bible tells us that people would wait by the pool for an angel to stir the water, and the first one in the water after the stirring was healed. Jesus came by the pool of Bethesda in this story, and saw a man sitting there waiting for the stirring of the water, hoping against hope that he could be the first one to make it in, and actually asked the man if he wanted to be healed.

The answer to this question would seem pretty obvious to most people. Who wouldn't want to be healed from their disability? Let's study deeper into the heart of the question Jesus was asking, as well as the heart of the man who said he wanted healing.

I believe that Jesus was asking a question much deeper than what was actually spoken here. At face value, this question wouldn't really need to be asked to most of us, if we had a physical problem. Of course we want to be healed! But, consider the fact that this man had been in this condition for thirty eight years. He had grown accustomed to sitting there waiting for something to happen. Upon his healing, he would have to learn a whole new way of life; working instead of begging; doing instead of setting; putting forth effort to live instead of waiting for someone to provide him a living. This man was within reach of a complete healing of his physical body, which would change his very way of life. Jesus presented him with this question; wanting the man to be sure he really wanted the healing that was available to him.

Jesus is asking men and women the very same question today, the same as He has asked forever. Do you want to be healed? While we may not be presented with a physical healing, the healing offered to us is much more important than our physical abilities. The healing offered to us is spiritual. Jesus has already provided this healing, and all that is left is for us to make the decision if we want it or not. He offers it to us on a daily basis; first, in salvation, and secondly, for our spiritual well-being.

At face value, we would all say yes to what is being offered. But just as Jesus was asking this man to consider the cost of a whole body, so must we consider the cost for the healing offered. For true healing, something is required of us. A change in the innermost parts of our heart must take place. Jesus wants to heal us, but we must be willing to change our ways. We must be willing to surrender to him our lives; our habits; our schedules; our loves; our desires; everything about us!

Many Christians today suffer spiritually, just as this man suffered physically. We tell Him we want the abundant life He offers, but we are unwilling to let Him change us! We want the growth without the rain. We want to be used in big ways by God, but refuse to be under the authority of pastors and teachers who can direct us towards that outcome in our lives.

Just as the man in this story would have to learn a different way of life, we have to learn to let God direct us and change things to match His plan for us. Many times, this will involve much pain, because we will have to let go of things we have grown accustomed to in life. The abundant life is a growing process, and we must present ourselves to the school master as trainable students if we want the healing of Christ; if we want to be usable to Him. We can't just sit around and wait for something to happen; we have to learn from Him and to do that, we must be teachable.

THE TRUE VINE

John 15:4-5, "Abide in me, and I in you, as the branch cannot bear fruit of itself, except it abide in the vine; no more can ye, except ye abide in me. I am the vine, ye are the branches: he that abideth in me, and I in him, the same bringeth forth much fruit: for without me ye can do nothing."

So many of us today get caught up in the idea that we have to do something, or be something important. When we look at our lives, we see what we can rightfully classify as a watered down Christianity. From time to time, we end up getting something right, and are blessed greatly by God, but for the most part, many Christians' lives are at best mundane and filled with struggles that we lose. Some of us keep trying, and failing, throughout life. Most, however, try a few times, but end up going back at least part way into our old lifestyle. There must be a reason for this failure in our lives.

In these verses, Jesus gives us essential information that we must understand if we want to have a successful and victorious life. He tells us to ABIDE in Him. Many Christians want to live a casual Christian lifestyle, calling upon Jesus only when we need His help with something. We go out and get in over our heads, and when we realize we are sinking, we frantically call out to Him to save us. But the picture Jesus gives us here as a vital element for our survival is that we are ALWAYS with Him. We spend time with Him on a daily basis, take Him to work with us, communicating with Him constantly during our day. We can own many houses, but we can only ABIDE in one. This house is where our treasures are; where we come home to at night. We must make Jesus the place we live; not just when we need something from Him, but every minute of every day.

Next, Jesus wants to abide in us. If we are truly saved, He is, and always will be, our Savior. But He wants so much more than that. In our homes, we will not allow anything inside that could damage them, or make them unlivable. When a person trusts Christ as their Savior, this Savior comes to abide in the person. He cannot abide where there is corruption! We must actively seek out those things that He hates, and abolish them from our lives! If you would not live in a house that is falling apart with the corruption of outside sources, why would you think your Savior would?

In the next phrase, Jesus qualifies His command in very simple terms. As Christians, we are to bear fruit. Never will you see any fruit coming from a branch that has been removed from a tree. A person can cut a branch from a tree and preserve it, but it will never again bear fruit. It immediately becomes useless for anything other than an ornament to decorate with.

It is very easy to become confused in this world about what the real key to success is. Twenty five people may well have twenty five different theories about what it takes to have a fruitful and happy life, but the simple fact is that we will be nothing more than decorations around the Church if we do not abide in Jesus Christ.

Then Jesus tells us that the person who abides in Him will bring forth MUCH fruit. So often we get started abiding in Him and begin to bear fruit until life becomes hard. When we find that the enemy has set his sights on us and brings hardships our way, it is very easy to lose focus and leave the true vine that gives us life and makes us fruitful. Or sometimes we may begin to believe that we are bearing fruit because of something we have done. Whatever the reason may be, when we begin to let the corruption back into our lives, we will soon start to wither away, because our life line will be severed.

We must constantly be on guard for anything in our lives that will begin to separate us from Jesus Christ. Even good things can become bad influences in our lives, if they are allowed to hinder our walk with Christ. The most important thing we can do as Christians is to commit to honor God in everything we do, making Him the most important and easily seen object in it.

A FILE IN GOD'S HANDS

Proverbs 27:17, "Iron sharpeneth iron; so a man sharpeneth the countenance of his friend."

In my shop, I have drawer that has many files. I also have an electric grinder sitting on the work bench. On top of the refrigerator, I have a steel that is used for sharpening knives. These tools all have something in common with one another; they were designed for specific purposes. In the right hands, and used with a constructive purpose in mind, they are great tools that can take very hard surfaces and alter their shape to make a tool that is very helpful. I use my grinder to sharpen my mower blades after they become dull and can no longer cut grass efficiently. I use the steel in the kitchen to take a knife that has become dull after much use, and I can put a razor edge on the knife blade.

However, used in hands that do not know how to use these files, grinders, and steels, much damage can be done to tools, making them utterly ineffective, and destroying any possibility that they can ever be used again. If one puts a knife blade on a steel the wrong way, instead of sharpening it, it would be made flat like the back side of the knife. If a grinder is used too long or hard on the mower blade, the temper will be removed from the blade, making the once hard metal soft and useless.

This verse tells us that we are like these tools that can be used to sharpen those around us. We can also be used to destroy those around us, making them ineffective in this life. Those we keep around us can also have either of these effects upon us!

God has given us His Word, showing us and giving us examples of how to use our lives for His glory and honor. He wants us to yield ourselves to His hands so that He can use us to mold those around us to a cutting edge that He can use. The way to this usefulness is simply stated, but sometimes hard to accomplish. A daily relationship of studying His Word and seeking His will for our daily lives is required to make us the effective files He wants us to be.

Each day we make a choice what we will be to Him. Will we yield to His masterful touch, letting Him sharpen us, and use us to sharpen others, or will we allow ourselves to go into the wrong hands to be used by the enemy to destroy those we love?

PERSECUTED FOR A PURPOSE

2 Corinthians 4:8-10, "We are troubled on every side, yet not distressed; we are perplexed, but not in despair; persecuted, but not forsaken; cast down, but not destroyed. Always bearing about in the body the dying of the Lord Jesus, that the life also of Jesus might be made manifest in our body."

Have you ever wondered why life is so hard? Why is it so hard to change a sinful lifestyle into one that honors God? Why is it so hard to love and serve Him? We serve a God that can do anything without even thinking about it; why does He not make our life easier to live for Him?

Many Christians get very discouraged when we face trials and persecutions. These verses can be a huge blessing to us as we travel into these times in our lives. When we face these huge obstacles in life and our enemy begins telling us that we have failed and that we cannot win, we must remember that Scripture promises us that we will have these problems in our lives. 2 Timothy 3:12 tells us, "Yea, and all that will live godly in Christ Jesus will suffer persecution." Satan wants us to believe that as a Christian, our lives should be filled with ease and luxury. Nothing could be farther from the truth! We are certain to have conflict in life if we are trying to live for God. Why? Because the world hates those who love God.

This should encourage us also for the fact that God has put us to the test. He wants to increase our strength and faith in Him, and these trials is how this happens. We can be troubled by the world, and often by family and friends, yet know that God has the ultimate control of our situation. We may not understand why something is happening to us, but at the same time we can trust that God is up to something to benefit us through it. When we are persecuted, we can rest in the fact that He will never leave us, and that He will give us the strength to endure without failing Him. And when our loved ones cast us away because of our faith, we can be certain that God will not allow us to be destroyed! We must endure these things in life, and God will give us the grace to do it, so "that the life also of Jesus might be made manifest in our body."

Verse 16 of this chapter says, "For which cause we faint not; but though our outward man perish, yet the inward man is renewed day by day. For our light affliction, which is but for a moment, worketh for us a far more exceeding and eternal weight of glory." If we commit our way to Him, no matter what happens, no matte what we may face in life, He will renew us every day. He will prepare us each morning for the day He knows we will face; and He will see us through it! Not only will He see us through it; He will give us victory, and make us better and fuller people.

PRECIOUS PROMISES

2 Peter 1:3-4, "According as His divine power hath given unto us all things that pertain unto life and godliness, through the knowledge of Him that hath called us to glory and virtue: Whereby are given unto us exceeding great and precious promises: that by these ye might be partakers of the divine nature, having escaped the corruption that is in the world through lust."

There are many times throughout life in which the Christian will find himself feeling lonely, abandoned, helpless, hopeless, and worthless, but the one thing he should remind himself in these times is that these feelings are lies of the enemy. They are often very effective lies, and ones the enemy uses over and over with great success. Satan knows that he is powerless in the face of Jesus Christ, but if he can blind the Christian to the truth that he is never without help, and never out of the reach of the Savior, he is certainly not powerless against the sheep who has lost sight of the Shepherd.

As hard as it gets to walk the walk of a Christian, the Lord has given you everything you need to live the Christian life with success. While you will never, in this lifetime, be sinless and without problems and struggles, if you can learn to lean on His strength and promises, you can live without being defeated by the sins you struggle with on a daily basis. Much to the contrary, if you cling to His power and promises, you will soon see more and more victory over these struggles in your life. As Peter found out, it is only when the Christian begins looking at things other than Jesus Christ that he begins to be overtaken by the waves of sin.

In those times when you begin to feel these attacks coming, there is strength to be drawn from the promises in God's Word. The first sentence in our text says that He has given us all things that pertain unto life and godliness. Take a moment and really consider this sentence. He has given all things that pertain to this present life, and for your spiritual life. There is nothing that you will ever need that will not be provided by God! The enemy will whisper in your ear that God does not love you; that He has forgotten about you. When you face terrible situations with painful outcomes, Satan will tell you to turn to sin because it will comfort you in your pain. When someone you trusted makes it clear to you that they cannot be trusted, Satan will tell you to strike back at them in any way possible. But God wants you to understand that even though these things catch you off guard and surprise you, threatening to destroy you, that He knows about it and He cares. He has not forgotten you; He is working to bring you closer to Him. The goal of your enemy is to destroy you; the goal of God is to give you life and godliness! How does He do that? By bringing you to a point in your life that you must call out to Him, trust Him through the hard times, and get to know Him better.

Instead of listening to your enemy's lies, try today to listen to God's promises.

- **When the enemy tells you God is letting things happen to bring about your destruction:**
  Jeremiah 29:11, "For I know the thoughts that I think towards you, saith the LORD, thoughts of peace, and not of evil, to give you an expected end."

- ***When the enemy tells you that you cannot do the things you should do:***
    Isaiah 40:29-31, "He giveth power to the faint; and to them that have no might He increaseth strength. Even the youths shall faint and be weary, and the young men shall utterly fall: But they that wait upon the LORD shall renew their strength; they shall mount up with wings as eagles; they shall run, and not be weary; and they shall walk, and not faint."

- ***When the enemy tells you that God cannot take care of you:***
    Philippians 4:19, "But my God shall supply all your need according to His riches in glory by Christ Jesus."

- ***When the enemy tells you that you cannot win the battle you are facing:***
    Romans 8:37-39, "Nay, in all these things we are more than conquerors through Him that loved us. For I am persuaded, that neither death, nor life, nor angels, nor principalities, nor powers, nor things present, nor things to come, nor height, nor depth, nor any other creature, shall be able to separate us from the love of God, which is in Christ Jesus our Lord."

Friend, you are in good hands when you are resting in the hands of God. He will never forsake you, He will never forget you, He will never put more on you than what you are able to get through by resting on His promises. Don't let your enemy talk you into walking away from your loving Heavenly Father!

DILIGENCE BRINGS FRUITFULNESS

1 Peter 1:5-8, "And beside this, giving all diligence, add to your faith virtue; and to virtue knowledge; and to knowledge temperance; and to temperance patience; and to patience godliness; and to godliness brotherly kindness; and to brotherly kindness charity. For if these things be in you, and abound, they make you that ye shall neither be barren nor unfruitful in the knowledge of our Lord Jesus Christ."

In 1 Peter 1:3-4, we are told of the precious promises given to us through Scripture that make us partakers of the divine nature; a nature that we certainly cannot attain without divine help. We know these promises are there, found throughout Scripture. We can read them over and over; we can memorize them; we can and should thank God for them. But the sad fact is that most Christians take the step into Christianity, then go on to live a life full of discouragement, loneliness, and failure, spending the rest of their lives wondering why this "Christian Life" didn't work for them.

It is true that God promises us victory over our sins. It is true that God promises to prosper us, in everything that we do. It is true that God promises to lead and guide us. But it is also true that God expects something more of us than just to take the salvation that He offers. The Christian who lives a defeated life lives that life in spite of God's wishes. The Christian who lives a life with no fruit lives that life in direct defiance to God's commands for him. The four verses in our context go a little farther into telling the Christian how he can experience an increase in the power of the divine nature in his life.

It starts by telling us that we should take the promises talked about in verses 3 and 4 and build upon them. First it talks about diligence. The Christian must be diligent (completely devoted and focused) upon this undertaking. It is true, the promises are there; but the Christian must take action upon them! You might have a million dollars in a bank account, but if you don't have a check book or debit card with you, you will never be able to buy anything. The same is true with all of the promises given to you in the Word of God. You must be diligent in your Christian walk, spending time with the Lord and meditating upon His Word, if you want to get the most out of what He gives you.

All of the following must be done with this diligence. Add to your faith. Everyone knows those Christians who seem to have everything all together. They seem to have such great faith, and often times the weak Christian longs to have the same faith. The fact of the matter is that no one has any more faith than anyone else. Romans 12:3 says that God has given each man the measure of faith. The key to the strength of your faith is how much you exercise it, or your lack of exercising it. The points in the next verses tells how to exercise it to increase its strength in your life.

First, the Christian is told to add <u>virtue</u>, or, moral excellence; goodness; righteousness. What good is a Christian who continues to live that same life that he lived before his relationship with Christ? God wants you do be diligent about living a good, clean life. He knows you cannot be perfect, and does not expect this; but He does expect you to live a righteous life for Him. To this virtue, the Christian should add <u>knowledge</u>. This knowledge should be a knowledge of God's Word. Too often Christians want the preacher and teacher to know what Scripture says, but think they are exempt from this requirement because they are "too busy" to be diligent about the study of God's Word. Friend, this verse doesn't tell the preacher to have knowledge; it tells you and me.

To this knowledge, the Christian should add <u>temperance</u>. This is moderation or self-restraint in action, statement, etc. This is talking about self-control. In this world today, self-control is almost unheard of. People are prideful and arrogant; we want what we want, and if we cannot have what we want, we like to have a temper tantrum. How can God possibly be expected to bless an individual like this? The Christian needs to learn what self-control is, and apply it to every aspect of his life. To this temperance, the Christian should add patience. Actually, these two go hand in hand. A person who learns self-control will also learn patience. God wants you to understand that sometimes you will have to wait for something; and He wants you to wait patiently.

And to patience, the Christian should add <u>godliness</u>. This is simply conforming to the laws and wishes of God. As you grow in your walk with the Savior, He will reveal more and more things in your life that He is not happy with. He wants you to be diligent to give up those things you like that displease Him. He also wants you to be diligent to add to your life some things that may displease you, but that please Him. He wants to show Himself to others through your life, and this requires a willingness to do what He wants, when He wants.

To godliness, the Christian needs to add <u>brotherly kindness</u>. Just as He wants others to see Him through your life, He also wants them to understand that He is a God who is nice. No one wants to be around someone who is hateful or bitter all the time. To brotherly kindness, the Christian should add <u>charity</u>, or love. He wants to love others through you. Throughout life, you will meet many who do not deserve to be loved. They will be hard for you to love. But remember, at one time you were very hard for someone else to love as well.

As you study these things, you will begin to understand that they are all progressive in your Christian walk. Without having a relationship with Christ, you will never be able to be a virtuous person. Without becoming this virtuous person, you will never be diligent about gaining knowledge of Scripture and of God. Someone who has no knowledge of God or the Bible will have no self-control; and he who has no self-control will not find it possible to be patient. He who is not patient will not be godly, and he that is not godly will never be kind to his brother.

If you stop being diligent on any one of these areas, you will stop growing in your Christian life. But verse eight says that if these things are found in you, you will be a fruitful Christian. Being fruitful will bring more peace and happiness in your life, and it will make those promises we talked about last time come very much alive in your life; "having escaped the corruption that I in the world through lust."

ENDING THE DESPAIR OF DOUBT

2 Peter 1:9-10, "But he that lacketh these things is blind, and cannot see afar off, and hath forgotten that he was purged from his old sins. Wherefore the rather, brethren, give diligence to make your calling and election sure: for if ye do these things, ye shall never fall."

This verse comes directly after the adding that is supposed to be done by the Christian. We have already seen in verses 5-8 that we are to "add to your faith virtue; and to virtue knowledge; and to knowledge temperance; and to temperance patience; and to patience godliness; and to godliness brotherly kindness; and to brotherly kindness charity. For if these things be in you, and abound, they make you that ye shall neither be barren nor unfruitful in the knowledge of our Lord Jesus Christ." We have also already seen what these additions add to the productivity and peace of our lives.

These verses go on to tell what happens to those who refuse to do the work associated with a spiritual relationship with the Lord Jesus Christ. Have you ever doubted your salvation? I'm not talking about a passing question that pops into your head, to be washed away when you answer, "yes!" I am asking about a doubt that keeps you from going to sleep at night, wakes you up once you do get to sleep, makes you unproductive at work, and makes you afraid to be alone.

This kind of doubt hit me in the summer of 1995. I was recently married, and had a great life to look forward to, but living a "Christian life" was the farthest thing from my mind. When this doubt hit me, there was nothing I could do to stop it, or even ease it. I would drop to my knees and beg God to save me, give me assurance of salvation, help me in some way; but no help came. The more I pleaded with God to help me, the more lost and desperate I became. Friend, if you have never been at this place, I can assure you that you never want to visit it. And if you have been there, you most assuredly never want to go back.

Why do so many true Christians live in verse nine, when the previous verses, if acted upon, will assure that they never have to understand what verse nine means? The Christian talked about in this verse is a true, born again Christian. But, because he has not been building upon the faith that was given to him, the verse says that he has become blind, cannot see afar off, and has forgotten that he has been purged from his old sins.

The faith that God gave you for salvation is just the beginning of the journey. It is just enough for you to realize the fact that you needed help in doing something that you cannot do; you needed a Savior. Because you had that faith, and acted upon it, guarantees you eternal life and forgiveness of your sins; but it is not enough to remove those sinful habits and addictions from your life. If you never add to your faith as talked about in these previous verses, you WILL come to a time in your life that you are not even sure you ever had that life-changing experience. At that time, the prayer of salvation will do you no good at all. It will change nothing in your life, and the more you try to gain assurance of your salvation, the worse you will be.

The Christian needs to follow the wonderful advice of verse 10, "Wherefore the rather, brethren, give diligence to make your calling and election sure: for if ye do these things, ye shall never fall." Remember, the word diligent means to be completely devoted and focused. How can you make your calling and election sure?

Many denominations will use this verse to question the reality of your eternal salvation. But your calling and election does not need to be made sure to God. This verse is talking about making it sure to us. Because of the fact that you let the Holy Spirit work in your life, changing what He doesn't like, and showing Himself through your life, you can look back on those days when that doubtful question blows through your mind, and be sure of your calling and election by God. It is only the Christian who doesn't build upon his faith that can be made to doubt what God has so miraculously done in his life.

Do you already have those doubts that you cannot seem to get rid of? The only way to get them gone is by practicing verses 5-8 in your life. Are there things in your life that you know shouldn't be there? Let God take them away, replacing them with Himself. Start building upon the faith that He has already given you; virtue; knowledge; temperance; patience; godliness; brotherly kindness; and charity. As you start letting God add these things to your life, you will find your doubts taking flight!

AN ENTRANCE OF HONOR

2 Peter 1:11-13, "For so an entrance shall be ministered unto you abundantly into the everlasting kingdom of our Lord and Saviour Jesus Christ. Wherefore I will not be negligent to put you always in remembrance of these things, though ye know them, and be established in the present truth. Yea, I think it meet, as long as I am in this tabernacle, to stir you up by putting you in remembrance;"

The previous verses in this chapter talk about diligently adding to your faith. The things a Christian should be adding to his faith are things that will cause him to have an ever closer walk with the Lord. Each day of life, the Christian should look and act a little more like his Savior. Each day of life the Lord should have more power and control in the life that He has given His own life for; power and control that will cause the world to see Christ as it looks at the Christian, seeing a life with meaning and direction.

Verse 10 ends by saying that if you will live your life this way, you will never fall. Verse 11 says that if you live with this diligence, giving Christ His rightful place in your life and letting Him live through you, an entrance with honor will be given to you when you finally enter heaven. If only the Christian could understand the trade that Christ wants to make with him! A life on this earth that is dark and dreary, filled with defeats and failures, but nevertheless, a life that one clings to and fights for, both physically and spiritually. And at the end of this life, all that has been fought for will be left behind for others to fight over. The trade offered in these verses is unimaginable to the human mind: Christ wants us to give to Him this life that we cannot hold on to—in exchange, He will grant us honor and glory, and entrance into an eternal life that we could never attain by ourselves.

In verse 12 and 13, Peter warns the reader that as long as he lives, he will be always reminding them of these truths, even though they know them already. The Christian of today also needs to be reminded many times of the implications of this chapter. The way in which the Christian lives his life today not only affects how his life will be tomorrow, but in eternity as well. The enemy has so many things to hinder your close walk with the Lord! Many of these things are very important for life, and are very easily used by Satan to get between you and your Savior. Many more are disguised simply as things designed to make life easier or more enjoyable.

You and I need to make sure we have people in our lives that are godly examples in our lives. We need to be reminded constantly that our life upon this earth, if we are Christians, are no longer ours, but now belong to Jesus Christ. Galatians 2:19-20 talk about the fact that Christ lives through us, and that He gave His life so that we might have life through Him. We have no right to ourselves, or to our desires. This is only one reason why it is so very important for the believer to go to Church and have godly friends who will hold him accountable for his actions.

Peter said, "I will not be negligent to put you always in remembrance of these things, though ye know them, and be established in the present truth." Even though we can say that we know this truth, and understand it, we can quickly turn from it as we get caught up in life and family problems today. Hebrews 10:25, "Not forsaking the assembling of ourselves together, as the manner of some is; but exhorting one another: and so much the more, as ye see the day approaching."

It is imperative that we not be negligent of our spiritual temperature. It is imperative that we have godly influences in our lives that will hold us on the right path. It is imperative that we use our lives as a godly influence to the weaker Christians in our lives. Even a strong and growing Christian can be led to ungodly paths very quickly, if he becomes anything short of diligent in building upon his faith, or if he allows the wrong people to influence him.

Who will by using your life to draw others today?

DEAD TO SIN

Romans 6:1-3, "What shall we say then? Shall we continue in sin, that grace may abound? God forbid. How shall we, that are dead to sin, live any longer therein? Know ye not, that so many of us as were baptized into Jesus Christ were baptized into His death?"

Why do the majority of Christians live a life of defeat? Why do so many of us hold onto our old sins? Why do we think we can trust God only enough to give us salvation, but we cannot get victory from our past lifestyle through Him? Why do so many of us not only live in continued sin, but make fun of it, and laugh at it? We say we have been "saved," but what have we really been saved from, if there is no difference in our lives?

Many Christians come onto the "Christian scene" with numerous deep seated sins. We have watched our Mom's and Dad's do the very things we do today. They did many of them secretly, while we do them openly. We have seen people the world thought of as "Men of God" crash and burn after their secret sins had been revealed to the world. As parents, we so often try to hide our sinful lifestyles from our children, only letting them see our great hypocrisy; there is no way to hide our true selves from those who know us so closely. In reality, we have grown up believing the lie that it is ok if we have sin in our lives. God loves us, knows we try, and will overlook our shortcomings, if only we mean well. So we live like our families before us, teaching our families after us, to live the same meaningless, sinful lives of misery and failure.

God expects, no, demands, more from us than this. It is by grace that we were saved. This is where grace abounds! After that very moment that we put our trust in God we became dead to sin. No more does satan and sin have power and dominion over us in this life. We are to serve a higher power; one who gives the knowledge, wisdom, and power to overcome the things in life that He is not pleased with. When we put our trust in Jesus Christ, we removed our trust from this world, and everything it offers. Because everything it offers is bondage and death.

Upon death, one loses everything he has accumulated throughout life. When we leave this world in death, we can certainly take nothing with us. It will not matter how much or how little we made. It will not matter what kind of house we lived in, or what we drove. Those things will all be over for us. This is exactly the picture these verses are making for us to understand.

Upon placing our faith in Jesus, we died to the things of this world; things that we had previously been alive to, and became alive to God's world; things we had previously been dead to. While the old man certainly clings to us, wanting to do the things he always has done, we have a new nature; a new man that is alive to the spiritual things God has for us. After we put our faith in Him, He expects us to also put our life in Him. Love what He loves. Hate what He hates. Live how He lived while upon this earth.

He is no longer here in body. He lives through us. We are to be an extension of Him. We are to show His power over sin in our lives. We are to point others to true life in Him. We say, "But it is so hard to change!" He says, in verse 7, "For he that is dead is freed from sin." Could it be the fact is really: it is not so hard to change, but just that we want to keep living in sin? If we really want the freedom He says is there, it shouldn't be so terribly hard to find it in our lives.

THE HEALER OF BETRAYAL

Psalm 41:9, "Yea, mine own familiar friend, in whom I trusted, which did eat of my bread, hath lifted up his heel against me."

Psalm 55:12-14, "For it was not an enemy that reproached me; then I could have borne it: neither was it he that hated me that did magnify himself against me; then I would have hid myself from him: But it was thou, a man mine equal, my guide, and mine acquaintance. We took sweet counsel together, and walked unto the house of God in company."

I have found few things in life that are comparable to being betrayed by someone I considered a very close friend, or someone I have confided in with the problems and discouragements in my life. Many people come and go through our lives, and it sometimes seems that we will spend an entire lifetime looking, with no success, for one true friend who we can walk with. Many are the times that we may think we have found that friendship we so desired, only to find out the hard way that they were never a true friend at all. Instead of the friend we thought we had, we find someone who wants nothing more than to destroy us.

It is even harder when you find that the person you have followed and learned from is the one who turns his back on you. How is it possible that the very person who has been used by God to teach and help train you becomes one who would do you harm? How can you continue growing in a Christian life when faced with these obstacles? Is it even possible to walk alone in this world, facing an enemy that you cannot see; an enemy that can very effectively use your once close friends against you?

Friend, this happens all the time in this world. Few things can devastate the life of a Christian more effectively than this. Few things can make a growing Christian turn back to his or her former lifestyle faster than this scenario. And if we focus on the wrong things when it happens to us, we can be guaranteed of one thing: our Christian life will fail miserably. Let's look at the solution to getting through this desperate time in life.

Isaiah 41:10, "Fear thou not; for I am with thee: be not dismayed; for I am thy God: I will strengthen thee: yea, I will help thee: yea, I will uphold thee with the right hand of my righteousness.

First and foremost, we must understand that we cannot get through this alone. The more we try to just go on with life, the more what has happened will consume us. This is not something that has happened by someone we didn't know; it has come from someone we trusted. We must learn to put our trust in God, even if the entire world is against us. Even though it may seem that we walk this life alone and rejected, we have a friend who will never leave us. Jesus will most certainly always be there, and He is able to provide the comfort we so desperately need in these times. It can never be in our power; what we need to get through this time can only come from Him. We have His promise that He will hold us—with His righteousness.

Romans 8:28, "For we know that all things work together for good to them that love God, to them who are the called according to His purpose."

Secondly, and also impossible for us to do without leaning upon God's righteousness, we must trust that God knows what is happening, and that He has a purpose for letting it happen. Though it has caught us completely by surprise, God can be surprised by nothing. Maybe He did not cause it to happen, but He has allowed it to happen for some specific purpose in our lives. He can take terrible things that happen to us and turn them around for our good, and for the good of others. But for this verse to work in our lives, we MUST continue to love and trust Him.

Proverbs 20:19, "He that goeth about as a talebearer revealeth secrets: therefore meddle not with him that flattereth with his lips."

We must also remove ourselves from the presence of those who would do us harm. Many times this is much harder to do than we would imagine. For one, this person was our friend, and we want to fix things. More often than not, these betrayals will come from those who are family members. But the more we try to fix things, the worse they will become. We must distance ourselves from these people, and ignore their accusations.

Exodus 14:14, "The Lord shall fight for you, and ye shall hold your peace."

We must simply let God fight for us. Even if it seems that everyone we know believes the lies that are being spoken, we cannot try to fight for ourselves. We must realize that we cannot fight our enemy. He is much stronger and smarter than we are. He has resources that we will never know about. God says that He will do our fighting for us. God cannot lose!

Romans 8:38-39, "For I am persuaded, that neither death, nor life, nor angels, nor principalities, nor powers, nor things present, nor things to come, nor height, nor depth, nor any other creature, shall be able to separate us from the love of God, which is in Christ Jesus our Lord."

We must understand that the intention of our enemy is to draw us away from the fact that God loves us, and wants the best for us. The enemy will attack us in the way that we are most vulnerable. He wants us to lose faith. He wants us to turn our back on God. He wants us to reject our loving Savior just as we have been rejected by others. He wants us to start placing blame on God because things are going wrong in our lives. But this verse says that NOTHING can separate us from the love of our Savior. We must cling to the friendship of Jesus Christ, even when every other friend in our life has gone.

Mark 10:27, "And Jesus looking upon them saith, with men it is impossible, but not with God: for with God all things are possible."

Lastly, and most importantly, we need to understand that we cannot make it through this in our own strength. It is not possible for us to be betrayed by those closest to us without it destroying us. So often we put our trust in Jesus for salvation, and think it ends there. We try to go on our own for the rest of the journey. We MUST lean upon His power. It is only He that can bring us through this time in our lives with more strength and more passion to live a life of righteousness.

THROUGH PEACE COMES VICTORY

Romans 5:1-2, "Therefore being justified by faith, we have peace with God through our Lord Jesus Christ: By whom also we have access by faith into this grace wherein we stand, and rejoice in hope of the glory of God."

So many Christians today who have come to Christ after a less than pleasant experience with major sin in their lives never learn to have victory in the big things they battle in life. The big things I refer to are peace with God, and learning to understand why they face tribulations and persecutions in life. Many believe that if they face tribulation, they must be doing something wrong. The fact is, the tribulation you are facing, and the trouble you are having in obtaining victory over a situation in life may very well be God's way of growing you as a Christian. Once you can understand this, it may well help you to be thankful during times of tribulation, which is what we talked about in the last devotion.

This passage begins by reminding the Christian that he is justified by faith. You and I know very well that we cannot be justified in God's eyes by our actions. Many of us have lived years in a sinful lifestyle. We have rejected the love of Christ many times, ignoring our friends and loved ones warnings to us, and paying no attention to God's own warnings through the preaching of His Word. We sin every day, and have nothing within ourselves that can justify us before God. But because of His love for us, He has made a way that we can stand before Him as justified and righteous people!

The justification we have through faith gives us peace with God. This is a wonderful gift from God to the sinner, but also one that the enemy loves to steal from us. Satan wants us to remember all the times we have failed, forgotten, rejected, and ignored God's desires for us. He will bring these things up as long as we will allow him to do so. Satan knows that he has lost control of your future when you turned to Christ, but he hopes to be able to hold you down in despair and discouragement by bringing up these failures again and again. Many times the Christian is kept by Satan from doing the work God has for him to do because he lives with a guilty conscience, thinking of the past sins he has committed; sins that have already been forgiven and forgotten by God. Don't let Satan steal your peace, and your future, by overloading your mind with false guilt from sins God doesn't even remember you have committed!!

Verse 2 goes on to say the faith that makes us justified in God's eyes is the same faith that gives peace with God and that gives the Christian access to the grace, or favor, of God. Think about the person you used to be before you met Jesus Christ. This person ran from God. This person was afraid of God. This person didn't want to hear about God's demands, or even His love. This is the person Satan wants you to think you still are. This is where your enemy wants you to live in your mind. But God has changed everything your enemy wants to use against you into something better!

If you have turned to Christ in faith, 2 Corinthians 5:17 says the old things of your life have passed away, and all things are new. God wants you to have peace. God wants you to rejoice in

145

His love, justification, and renewing power in your life. The choice, as always, is completely up to you. You can allow the lies of Satan to hold you back from what God wants you to be and do today, or you can rejoice in the fact that God has forgiven you of your past, and even wants to use your past for His glory.

If you have never yet turned to Christ in faith, you can do so right now. He will take the guilt of your sins away; and help you live the life that you never thought possible. He will forgive you, and make your future worth living for! He is able to take away those sins you battle every day. Turn to Him in faith, confessing to Him that you have sinned, and ask Him to save you and change you. You will never be sorry you did! Romans 10:13, "For whosoever shall call upon the name of the Lord shall be saved."

FROM TRIBULATIONS TO EXALTATIONS

Romans 5:1-2, "Therefore being justified by faith, we have peace with God through our Lord Jesus Christ: By whom also we have access by faith into this grace wherein we stand, and rejoice in hope of the glory of God."

So many Christians today who have come to Christ after a less than pleasant experience with major sin in their lives never learn to have victory in the big things they battle in life. The big things I refer to are peace with God, and learning to understand why they face tribulations and persecutions in life. Many believe that if they face tribulation, they must be doing something wrong. The fact is, the tribulation you are facing, and the trouble you are having in obtaining victory over a situation in life may very well be God's way of growing you as a Christian. Once you can understand this, it may well help you to be thankful during times of tribulation, which is what we talked about in the last devotion.

This passage begins by reminding the Christian that he is justified by faith. You and I know very well that we cannot be justified in God's eyes by our actions. Many of us have lived years in a sinful lifestyle. We have rejected the love of Christ many times, ignoring our friends and loved ones warnings to us, and paying no attention to God's own warnings through the preaching of His Word. We sin every day, and have nothing within ourselves that can justify us before God. But because of His love for us, He has made a way that we can stand before Him as justified and righteous people!

The justification we have through faith gives us peace with God. This is a wonderful gift from God to the sinner, but also one that the enemy loves to steal from us. Satan wants us to remember all the times we have failed, forgotten, rejected, and ignored God's desires for us. He will bring these things up as long as we will allow him to do so. Satan knows that he has lost control of your future when you turned to Christ, but he hopes to be able to hold you down in despair and discouragement by bringing up these failures again and again. Many times the Christian is kept by Satan from doing the work God has for him to do because he lives with a guilty conscience, thinking of the past sins he has committed; sins that have already been forgiven and forgotten by God. Don't let Satan steal your peace, and your future, by overloading your mind with false guilt from sins God doesn't even remember you have committed!!

Verse 2 goes on to say the faith that makes us justified in God's eyes is the same faith that gives peace with God and that gives the Christian access to the grace, or favor, of God. Think about the person you used to be before you met Jesus Christ. This person ran from God. This person was afraid of God. This person didn't want to hear about God's demands, or even His love. This is the person Satan wants you to think you still are. This is where your enemy wants you to live in your mind. But God has changed everything your enemy wants to use against you into something better!

If you have turned to Christ in faith, 2 Corinthians 5:17 says the old things of your life have passed away, and all things are new. God wants you to have peace. God wants you to rejoice in

His love, justification, and renewing power in your life. The choice, as always, is completely up to you. You can allow the lies of Satan to hold you back from what God wants you to be and do today, or you can rejoice in the fact that God has forgiven you of your past, and even wants to use your past for His glory.

If you have never yet turned to Christ in faith, you can do so right now. He will take the guilt of your sins away; and help you live the life that you never thought possible. He will forgive you, and make your future worth living for! He is able to take away those sins you battle every day. Turn to Him in faith, confessing to Him that you have sinned, and ask Him to save you and change you. You will never be sorry you did! Romans 10:13, "For whosoever shall call upon the name of the Lord shall be saved."

WAIT FOR THE PROMISE

Acts 1:4-5, " And, being assembled together with them, commanded them that they should not depart from Jerusalem, but wait for the promise of the Father, Which, saith He, ye have heard of me. For John truly baptized with water; but ye shall be baptized with the Holy Ghost not many days hence."

So often, we see people come out of a sinful lifestyle, having a truly changed heart, full of excitement and ready to do something for the Lord, only to see them a short time later back in their past lifestyle of sin. One automatically wonders if the person had a true salvation experience, but this is not for us to judge. What we would all do well to do is to study the formula for victory and a strong Christian life that cannot fail.

Jesus clearly had a job for the disciples to do. He had been training them and pouring His life into them for years, preparing them for the day that He would no longer walk the earth. But it was more important to Him that they wait upon Him than that they should just go out and get started with their mission. He told them to wait; not to try to do anything until they had received power from on high.

Over and over the Bible gives us instruction on how to have a strong, victorious Christian life. It warns us in Luke 14:28-30 not to start building something without having the funds to finish what we started. It tells in Luke 14:31-32 the wisdom of knowing the strength of our enemies before going to war with them. And in Luke 14:33, Jesus tells us the qualifications of being a disciple; we must forsake all and follow Him.

Jesus wants our service to Him, but there is something more important than service: that is obedience. 1 Samuel 15:22 tells us, "to obey is better than sacrifice, and to hearken than the fat of rams." We can never expect the Lord to accept our sacrifices in life if we do not first obey Him.

So what is the key ingredient to getting started in a life that honors God? Where do we need to start our new Christian walk in order that we may please God, and have His blessing and power on our lives? This is what we are each searching for, but very few have the patience to do what is necessary to achieve it. Jesus told the disciples to wait. Not to go out and get busy, or to try hard to please Him, or even to try right away to build something great for Him. Simply wait.

But waiting does not mean that we are not to be doing something. The key idea of waiting is not what we generally think of the word. The idea is to be available to the Lord. We should wait, not idly for God to do something with us, or to remove our addictions and strongholds, but to wait for His power by reading and meditating on His Word. Wait prayerfully for Him to reveal His direction and plan for our lives.

Too many times we chase a desire that we think is a good goal, only to find out that the enemy has planted a stumbling stone in our path. If we would but wait on God to give us His true direction, His true plan, and His power, our enemy would find us unstoppable. The disciples waited patiently upon Him in this very way, and the Church sprang up; in God's time, and in God's way. He will do the same for us!

Acts 1:14, "These all continued with one accord in prayer and supplication, with the women, and Mary the mother of Jesus, and with His brethren." They waited in prayer and meditation until God put His power upon them, and then were moved in His direction. If we want to have true victory and strength in our lives, we must follow this example!

THE RIGHT GOSPEL

Galatians 1:6-9, "I marvel that ye are so soon removed from Him that called you into the grace of Christ unto another gospel: which is not another; but there be some that trouble you, and would pervert the Gospel of Christ. But though we, or an angel from heaven, preach any other gospel unto you than that which we have preached unto you, let him be accursed. As we said before, so say I now again, if any man preach any other gospel unto you than that ye have received, let him be accursed."

Why is it so very easy to lay aside the Gospel that brought us true meaning in our lives? Why do we so often find ourselves ignoring what we have learned through the study of God's Word, and going back to the ways of the world? Why do we find ourselves trying to find a better way than what the Scriptures teach, or thinking we have to put "our spin" on the message, to reach others, or even to keep ourselves involved?

Paul said, "I marvel" not only that this has happened, but that it has happened so soon. The meaning of this word is "to wonder in astonishment." Paul almost couldn't believe how quickly this had happened to the Galatians. He knew their background. The Galatians had come from barbarians who had come to Greece in the third century before Christ. They had a lawless and meaningless ancestry. The teachings of Scripture had brought order from their chaos. The love and discipline brought to them through the Gospel message had made them no longer a people of rebellious spirit, but had shown them how to live in peace and harmony with one another. It had changed their people from a warring people to a loving and giving race. And yet, they had rejected the life and freedom giving Gospel for a legalistic religion; a religion that relies not upon Jesus for salvation, but upon their own righteousness!

As we look at what had transpired there, we can easily see why Paul was "marveling" at the change that had taken place. How could these, of all people, look to their ability to uphold the Law of God? But so many Christians today end up on the same road. God has brought us from a life of sin that was destroying our families, our bodies, and anyone who got too close to us. He has traded us our death for His life, and wants us only to love Him and live for Him. How can we, who were destined for destruction a very short time ago, begin to ignore His love and compassion for us?

He teaches us in His Word that He gives freedom. We have proved with our lives that when left to ourselves, we only make a mess of things. But so many take of His love and life changing power, only to wander off again and follow the lies of the world. If He has the power to save and to heal, He also has the power to teach us how to have a better life; how to remain free in a world that offers only bondage.

The people of Galatia had fallen for the lie that they could have the blessings of God by doing things their way. God wants you to understand that the freedom you started enjoying as a result of submitting to His Word will only be retained by a continuance in His Word. You must never stop learning of and from Him! You must never let anyone lead you to believe that there is a better way! Jesus Christ, and His teachings, is the ONLY WAY TO A FREEDOM THAT WILL LAST FOR ETERNITY!

If you will continue to study and love Him, He will continue to produce true freedom and peace; such as you have never known. Your live will only get sweeter and more meaningful with Him at the forefront. As you learn more about what He wants from you, He will give you more strength and grace to live the life that you simply cannot live without His power.

As you commit your life more and more to Him, you will also be faced with more and more chances to lay Him aside, just as the Galatians did. It is today that you make the choice what you will do!

1 Peter 5:7-8, "Casting all your care upon Him; for He careth for you. Be sober, be vigilant; because your adversary the devil, as a roaring lion, walketh about, seeking whom he may devour." Don't make the mistake of laying aside the truth of Jesus Christ for the lies of the devil.

JUSTIFIED BY WHAT?

Galatians 2:16, "Knowing that a man is not justified by the works of the law, but by the faith of Jesus Christ, even we have believed in Jesus Christ, that we might be justified by the faith of Christ, and not by the works of the law: for by the works of the law shall no flesh be justified…"

This passage of Scripture is vital for the person who seeks to be right with God to understand. So often, we hear people say that they try to do right, and hope that their good outweighs their bad at the end of life; they live their whole life hoping to be good enough to go to heaven. Many in the Church today are victims of this lie of the devil. He will tell us that we are good enough. He will tell us that we are much better people than many we see in the church. He will tell us that no one can follow the Law completely, and we just have to do the best we can do. He is right about one thing; no person alive can fulfill the Law of God!

We must understand that God never gave man His Law so that we could follow it and go to heaven. Its purpose was met immediately upon its deliverance to mankind. The only purpose of God's Law is to show us that we cannot measure up to God's standards. As I look at the Ten Commandments, I see things that I cannot possibly follow without ever failing even one of them. And yet, I must also understand that this Law must be satisfied in my life if I ever hope to have a relationship with God; and more than that: if I hope to ever arrive in heaven upon my death. God demands perfectness in a person's life.

So what shall we do to be right with God? The answer is simple, once we get around the thought that we can do something to earn our salvation! The way to a correct relationship with God is to put our faith and trust in Jesus Christ. Romans 3:23 tells us that every person alive today is born into sin. It doesn't matter how much or how little I sin; the truth is that I sin, and you sin. This fact puts everyone in the same condition. A lie, to God, is no worse or better than a murder. In His eyes, if we break one commandment, we have broken them all. There is nothing we can do to undo this fact! Romans 6:23 tells us what our sin has earned us; eternal separation from God, in hell. But then it tells about a gift that God has given us; His Son. This gift allows us to have eternal life; this gift allows us to have a restored relationship with our Creator! Romans 10:9-10 tells us how to receive this gift; confess (or, agree with God) that Jesus is the Way, the Truth, and the Life, and believe with all our heart that Jesus came to die for our sins, and came back from the dead on the third day.

"Even we have believed in Jesus Christ, that we might be justified by the faith of Christ.." It is not, now, nor was it ever, the Law that made men right with God! The Law only condemns. The Law shows us how far removed we are from the grace and blessings of God. It is only by turning our eyes from ourselves, and onto Jesus Christ, that we will ever be right with God. The word "justified" means, "Just as if we have never sinned." Jesus is willing to cover our sins with His perfect blood, shed upon the cross of Calvary, so that we might have the opportunity to know the Father's love for us!

It is time for us to start looking at the Son of God to give us righteousness, and stop looking at our works. As we look to Him, realizing the fullness of what He has done for us, we will realize a love so strong for Him that we will be unwilling to keep our hidden sins tucked away in our lives. It is not until we truly look to Him that we will see true freedom in our lives. Until then, we are slaves to the very thing that was intended by God to bring us to Him in repentance. Don't allow the lies of satan to make you believe that you can please God any other way than to look at His Son, and only His Son.

A LIFE THAT LIVES

Galatians 2:19-21, "For I through the law am dead to the law, that I might live unto God. I am crucified with Christ: nevertheless I live; yet not I, but Christ liveth in me: and the life which I now live in the flesh I live by the faith of the Son of God, who loved me, and gave Himself for me. I do not frustrate the grace of God: for if righteousness come by the law, then Christ is dead in vain."

Paul, in verse 16, told us that no person is justified by the Law. He starts this verse out explaining exactly what has happened to the person by the Law, just as it was intended to do. Because of the Law, we come to understand what we are truly worthy of; we come to understand how worthless we really are. As I look at the Law of God, given thousands of years ago to Moses, and really start to understand what it is showing me, I find out that I am hopelessly dead because of my sins. I have broken every one of the laws of God in some way or another! Here, the Law has fulfilled its purpose. I have no way available in and of myself to come to God. The Law has made me fully aware of how dead I am; that I might look to Jesus for the justification that I so desperately need.

I've heard it said many times that someone can't be saved until they are lost. We must come to this point in our lives before we will look to God for help. We have been told by society, and unfortunately, many in the church that we can get where we want to be if we try hard enough. My friend, just the opposite is true in the life of every person alive today! We have to come to the end of ourselves! We have to come to the conclusion that there is absolutely nothing we can do to save ourselves! We have to become dead before Jesus Christ can make us alive!

Paul then says that he is crucified with Christ. We have to be willing to lay our lives at the feet of Jesus if we want His help. We have to put down our dreams, our goals, our desires, and pick up His. Once we start doing this, and it is an everyday process; many times we will find we have to do it several times a day, we will see an amazing thing happen in our lives; we will truly start to live! We have to be willing to die to ourselves, so that He can give us true life and freedom from the sins that we struggle with constantly. It is not in our power, as we find again and again by looking at the Law; it is only by and through His power that this happens!

Lastly, Paul says that he does not frustrate the grace of God. So many times people are finally willing to give up on themselves and look to Jesus Christ for salvation, but within a very short amount of time, they seem to forget that the strength is not within them to live the life Christ wants them to live. They soon start trying to serve and please Him in their own power. Many Christians today want to go back to the Law and demand that people live by the very thing that "killed" them to begin with. They think that by upholding the Law they are pleasing God, and living a life that glorifies Him, when in reality, they are ignoring God, and trying to live a life of self-righteousness. Not only is this sinful, but it turns others away from God and His love for them.

If we are not righteous enough to earn our salvation, then how could we possibly be righteous enough to keep it? It is God that gives salvation, and it is God that retains salvation! We will never earn justification; it is a gift from a loving God. It was never God's goal or desire to make us follow the Law to be right with Him. He knows we could not ever meet His demands. He gave the Law for one reason; to make us realize that we are dead to Him until we look to Jesus Christ for our need.

Once gaining this justification, our job as a forgiven sinner is to live a life that points others not to look at how good we are, but to look at the One who gave us back the life we never knew possible. If we only continue looking to Him in faith, He will live His life through us, giving us victory over the strongholds in our lives, and pointing others to faith in Him. Then, we will be able to say with Paul, "I am crucified with Christ: nevertheless I live; yet not I, but Christ liveth in me: and the life which I now live in the flesh I live by the faith of the Son of God, who loved me, and gave Himself for me."

Let's give up trying to please Him in our own power, and just let Him live through us a life that points our friends and family to the life-giver.

WEARINESS OR PRODUCTIVENESS

Galatians 6:9-10, "And let us not be weary in well doing; for in due season we shall reap, if we faint not. As we have therefore opportunity, let us do good unto all men, especially unto them who are of the household of faith."

Any adult knows the devastating power of discouragement, either in a job, a family, or a relationship. As the seed of discouragement is planted, and allowed to grow, it soon takes over every aspect of life in whatever area it is in. If it is not dealt with quickly, it will ruin the job, the family, or the relationship, because it becomes the overpowering point of focus, outshining even the good things.

The Christian life is no different; we could go so far as to say discouragement is much worse in the life of a Christian who allows it to grow than in the life of the unbeliever. In our lives, it has the power to make us blind to our Savior. Instead of seeing the blessings of life; instead of seeing the godly qualities in a situation, a job, or a person; instead of seeing God working behind the scenes in these things, we begin to see only the bad. If not dealt with immediately, this discouragement will begin to grow into resentment, and even hatred.

Not only should the Christian use this verse as an encouragement in living the Christian life, there are many others to be found throughout Scripture that can be used to very effectively battle discouragement in life. This verse tells us to not be weary in well doing. In this world where so many people face so many problems, it is extremely easy to reach the point where one just stops trying to live this life that is so difficult. But the one who keeps on going for Christ no matter the cost has a promise from God to have fruit to show for their labors.

Anyone who has, or is, battling habitual sins/addictions in life also quickly tire of the continual fight to do what is right. The sin you battle the most in life has a way of becoming the focal point in your life. One day, week, or month is a good one, and if you are not constantly aware of how easy it is to let your guard down, that good day, week, or month might just be the last of many. Instead of thinking of the sin you battle, and how hard it is to overcome and keep the victory, you should be thinking of the reaping season that will soon come; that day when God has given complete victory over the area in your life that can so easily overpower you today.

Another wonderful verse we can turn to is Galatians 5:1, "Stand fast therefore in the liberty wherewith Christ hath made us free, and be not entangled again with the yoke of bondage." Your enemy wants you to focus on those discouraging and disheartening things in life because he wants to retain the power over you that he once had. Before being saved, you served him and him alone. He disguised it as many things, like doing whatever you wanted to do or being whoever you wanted to be. But the truth is that you were in bondage to his desires, his wants for you. Upon being saved, the Bible tells us that he no longer has any say about us. He no longer has any power over us, except what we allow him to have.

Satan doesn't care what you are in bondage to as a Christian, as long as he can find something that can hold you down. But Jesus Christ has given you victory over every sin that once had control of your life. You have only to claim that victory, and to retain it. How is the Christian to retain something that he has never been able to have in life before his relationship with Christ? Again, the focus must change! Before Christ became a part of your life, you were focused on your life, and those around you. If victory was given at the time of salvation, and salvation is obtained through Jesus Christ, it is Jesus Christ that you must keep your focus on!

Romans 8:15 tells us, "For ye have not received the spirit of bondage again to fear; but ye have received the Spirit of adoption, whereby we cry, Abba, Father." You see, God knows something that most Christians live their whole lives not understanding; we cannot live the Christian life in our own power. We are corrupted; we are broken individuals, and nothing good can come from us. This is why, upon salvation, He has given us the vital tool of the Holy Spirit.

It is not within our grasp to live this life without becoming weary. It is not possible for us to do good to others when they do us wrong. It is not possible for us to achieve victory over the sins and discouragements in our lives. As soon as we try to overcome these things in our own power, our focus shifts from He who makes life worth living to the thing that takes the life out of us. We MUST learn to let the Spirit work in our lives.

It all comes down to focus; what we focus on is what we will see, and what we will become. Will you allow Jesus Christ to be the focal point in your life today, making changes and bringing you to and through places He knows you need to go, or will you decide to keep trying to do it in your own power, and fail?

LIVING IN THANKSGIVING

Colossians 3:15-17, "And let the peace of God rule in your hearts, to the which also ye are called in one body; and be ye thankful. Let the word of Christ dwell in you richly in all wisdom; teaching and admonishing one another in psalms and hymns and spiritual songs, singing with grace in your hearts to the Lord. And whatsoever ye do in word or deed, do all in the name of the Lord Jesus, giving thanks to God and the Father by Him."

Every Christian alive today has the power to make a choice to let the peace of God rule in their lives. No matter what your life is like today; no matter how much chaos you endure on a daily basis, you can have peace from your Heavenly Father. This passage says to let His peace rule in your heart. It goes on to say, "And be ye thankful." We know that Scripture teaches us to live with a thankful spirit towards God, and know that God's Word would have us to be thankful not only through the hard times of life, but also for the hard times.

God never loses control of any situation. Nothing ever catches Him by surprise. He is always working in the life of a Christian! You may not be able to see Him working today, but you can rest assured that He is behind the scenes, making sure that what is allowed into your life today is designed to make you a better, stronger Christian.

And as always, the passage taken out of the Word of God for today does not tell us to do something and leave us with no idea how to accomplish it. We have read the command; now we will look at how to make this passage come alive in our hearts on this great Thanksgiving morning.

"Let the Word of Christ dwell in you richly in all wisdom." No matter if you have woken this morning to no problems, or many problems, in your life, you are told to let the Word of Christ dwell in you richly. Start the day today by meditating on His Word, not only today, but every day. He has all wisdom and power to get you through the problems you will face today, but if you have spent no time in His Word, you may not be able to remember the things you need to remember.

The next key factor in letting the peace of God rule in your heart is to be willing to teach those around you, and to be taught by those around you. Many people fail in this area because of stubbornness, known by God as pride. We must have a heart willing to hear correction and direction from those God has placed in our life. The first thing the heart wants to do when someone confronts us about something is to swell up with this pride and refuse to let the Holy Spirit correct us and direct us through this person. If this is the attitude we have today, there will be no peace from God.

Next, we see that we are to have a heart that is full of praise to the Lord. Even in the toughest circumstances we face in life, God wants us to be willing to praise Him. Have you taken time this morning to sing a song in your heart to the One who died to give you freedom today? We all know how quickly our mood changes from bad to good when our favorite song comes on the radio. God can, and will, use songs of praise coming from our hearts to make a terrible day much easier to get through.

Finally, we can see that we are to do everything today in the name of the Lord. Think about the things you plan to do on this day. If you will devote this day to Him, determined to make Him happy with your life today, how many of the things on your agenda would be forced to change?

These are the secrets to living a life ruled by the peace of God.

GIVE OF YOUR NOTHING

Luke 21: 1-4, "And He looked up, and saw the rich men casting their gifts into the treasury. And He saw also a certain poor widow casting in thither two mites. And He said, of a truth I say unto you, that this poor widow hath cast in more than they all: For all these have of their abundance cast in unto the offerings of God: but she of her penury hath cast in all the living that she had."

Often are the times we catch ourselves looking at the things others have, wishing that we could "have a better chance" at life. We see the highlights of these peoples' lives, and see nothing but glamour and easy living. As we look at others, why is it that we take the highlights of their lives and compare them with the lowest times of ours? Why can't we understand what we are truly seeing: the best of a life that has just as many problems as ours? Each person living today has troubles and problems that they just can't seem to find answers for. Each person living today has bad days and good days, times with little or no money, and times with enough. There is not a person alive today that does not have some regrets in their life.

If we, as Christians, and people coming out of the bondage of sin and addictions are not very careful, our enemy will sidetrack us, and eventually defeat us with this one simple tactic. He knows that if he can get us to turn our eyes from Jesus for only a second, he can get the foothold in our lives that he is looking for. From that foothold, our lives will only get worse.

Some people think back on the years that they lived away from God and wish they could have them back to do over again, serving God. The only thing this accomplishes is wasting yet another day. God does not want what you were yesterday. He is not trying to get you to serve Him, or even see Him yesterday. Yesterday is over. He is not trying to get you to serve Him or worship Him tomorrow. He wants you today. He wants your whole heart today. The cares and concerns of tomorrow so often make us worthless today.

You may think that you can't do much today, and if you could only get a better job, or at a better position in life you could serve and love Him more effectively then. This is a lie from satan. God wants you to love Him with your whole heart right now. Let Him worry about tomorrow.

In this passage, Jesus is trying to get the disciples to understand that it is not what someone does, or what they give, that God uses and appreciates. It is God that has given you whatever talents you possess. It is God that has provided you with the abilities you have. He wants you to be willing to give them to Him, no matter how big or small they are. There is nothing that our God cannot accomplish. He doesn't need your money, or your abilities. What He is looking for is a heart that is willing to give all that it has. Once He has this from your life, the possibilities are endless.

Don't be a victim to the lie that if you had more money you would start giving or helping. Don't be deceived into thinking that if you just weren't so busy, you would go to Church or spend time helping someone in desperate need. Luke 16:10 says, "He that is faithful in that which is least is faithful also in much: and he that is unjust in the least is unjust also in much."

What is it that you have been holding back from the Lord? What does He want from you? It doesn't matter at all to Him that it is not worth much in your eyes. He fed five thousand with five loaves and two fish. He fed four thousand with seven loaves and just a few fish. He washed away the sins of everyone who will ever believe on Him through one death.

It is not the quantity of what you possess that He is interested in; it is the quality with which you present it for His use. If you will but determine in your heart that what you have will be freely given to Him, He will take care of the rest. And it is with this one commitment that you will truly begin to be blessed beyond measure by God.

ABIDE WITH US

Luke 24: 28-31, "And they drew nigh unto the village, whither they went: and He made as though He would have gone further. But they constrained Him, saying, Abide with us: for it is toward evening, and the day is far spend. And He went in to tarry with them. And it came to pass, as He sat at the table with them, He took bread, and blessed it, and brake it, and gave to them. And their eyes were opened, and they knew Him; and He vanished out of their sight."

The men in this story had just been through the hardest time of their lives. The Man they had followed for years, learning from and living with, had just been brutally murdered, and along with Him, their dreams and hopes; their very lifestyle. All they had been taught; all they had been living for; died with Jesus Christ. As Christ's disciples, even their lives were worth less than nothing. They were assuredly scared they would meet the same fate if they were seen and caught by the rulers.

Many are the times in life that we will see our dreams and hopes vanish before our eyes. The things we were focused on will seemingly be proven wrong. The vision we had will be found to be false. The people, or person, we were following will be found a liar. It is in these times that we will make the most crucial decisions in our Christian life. It is also in these times that the temptation to revert back into our old lifestyle will be the most difficult to withstand. Any time one finds that he has believed a lie, and helped to spread that lie, he will undoubtedly question many things; his judgment, his values, the meaningfulness of his very life. If he can be sucked into someone's trickery, how important is he to the world anyway?

There is so much we can learn from the failures of the disciples; but even more lessons can be found from the things they did right! Even in the midst of this terrible time for them, they continued to live the teachings of Jesus Christ, even though they may not have realized it. The lessons learned from following Christ had taken root in their hearts, and His teachings were being lived out on the road to Emmaus.

Even in a world that hated everything they believed, they were still willing to walk and talk with strangers. They spent much time in conversation with someone they had never seen before, without even a thought that they might be talking with someone that would betray them. When they had come to the end of their journey, they could easily have told this stranger goodbye, without even considering his needs; with everything they had been through, who would have blamed them for this? But we see that they "constrained" Him to "Abide with us." This stranger knew they were suffering emotionally and didn't want to cause them any trouble, and tried to go on ahead, but they wouldn't take no for an answer. The day was over, and they knew He needed a place to sleep, and something to eat. If they had let Him go on like He would have done, they would not have realized the truth that night. They would have spent yet another night worrying about nothing.

It is often through the terrible times in life that the Lord works in miraculous ways for us.

If we will continue to live as He has given example, we can rest assured that He will never be far from us. Many times, it is God Himself that leads us into these times. They are designed to test and increase our faith. They are designed to make us rely on Him instead of ourselves. They are designed to break our pride and stubbornness and force us to come to Him.

But He will never force us to "take the high road" in life. Jesus would have kept walking that night if they had not been willing to put His needs before their own. The same is true for us. It is these times in life that we need to seek Him out even when it is as though He cannot be found. Search, and search some more. Determine in your heart that His way is the best way, even if the whole world is seeking to destroy you. Constrain Him to come and abide with you, and you will never go wrong. Give up on Him; go your own way, and you will never be right.

WISDOM FOR LIFE

James 1:5-6, "If any of you lack wisdom, let him ask of God, that giveth to all men liberally, and upbraideth not; and it shall be given him. But let him ask in faith, nothing wavering. For he that wavereth is like a wave of the sea driven with the wind and tossed."

Many people spend their lives with no wisdom ever applied to it. We know what God says is right, and wrong, but somehow just can't wrap our minds around how to do what we know we are supposed to be doing.

We go from one failure to another, losing a little more hope each time. We seek counsel and guidance from others who face the same shortcomings that we face ourselves. We keep hoping that one day we will happen to make the right choices and succeed in life.

The problem with this is the fact that we, in our flesh, are hopeless to make decisions based upon wisdom and righteousness. Our flesh will always follow satan. If we let our mind rule us, we will be forever hopeless. God's wisdom cannot be beaten. We cannot understand His wisdom, or His ways of doing things. This is why we just have to follow the Spirit. We must get our wisdom, not from others, but from Him.

We need to seek our guidance and counsel from the One who made us. He looks upon us, and yearns for us to come to Him. He is willing and totally able to help us with the problems and decisions we face. He longs to take our hand and help us up. He desires to feed us from His table, and clothe us with attire fitting for royalty.

But we must ask for it. And we must decide to abide by it. Wisdom is applied Knowledge. We must get the right kind of knowledge, from God's Word, and then we must ask for the strength from God to obey His Word. We must seek His face, His guidance. He must become the center point of our lives. Once He is in His rightful place, we will no longer be tossed around by the storms of life. Our faith must rest upon the Creator.

WHAT WISDOM WILL DO IN YOUR LIFE

Proverbs 1:5, "A wise man will hear, and will increase learning; and a man of understanding shall attain unto wise counsels."

There are many ideas about what makes a man or a woman wise. Many people think that much knowledge makes us wise. But as I look around, I see many people who have much education, who simply cannot be considered wise people. The Bible defines a wise person as one who knows what the Word of God teaches, and takes heed to it. Again, many people know the Word of God, or at least key parts of it, but very few people today learn from it, and obey it. This verse has a few key parts to it.

The very first thing a wise man does is hear. We simply cannot be wise if we refuse to hear the Word of God; the Spirit of God. He wants to talk to us, teach us, guide us, lead us. He is perfectly able to do all of these things, if only we will let Him do so. But He will never force us! We see time after time in Scripture where He pleads with us to accept His ways for us. He is the author and creator of our lives, and He knows what is best for us. He knows what we need for life; He knows what we need through life. And He wants to guide our lives for us, but we must first hear Him.

The second thing is to increase in learning. Many people graduate from High School and think they have learned everything they will ever need to know. Many in the church have been there for many years, have heard all the Bible stories, and think there is nothing left for them to learn from them. But nothing could be farther from the truth! The day we stop learning is the day we start dying; if not physically, than spiritually. There is always some other truth to learn from the Bible. There is always a deeper level of truth than we have attained to. We can find proof of this in the life and ministry of Paul, who before his transformation, was named Saul. He had been brought up and taught as a Pharisee, a group that prided themselves in the knowledge and devotion to the Law. He knew the Laws of God inside and out, and he thought he had no reason for further knowledge. Then he came to know the Lord Jesus Christ, and he began to understand that all that knowledge was useless unless he learned what God wanted him to know. He spent the rest of his life increasing in knowledge by the leading of the Holy Spirit, and was used by God to write over half of the New Testament!

The third thing is to attain unto wise counsels. What would it benefit our lives if we were able to train our ears, as well as our minds, to hear everything, if we never used what we heard for the betterment of our lives or the world around us? What would it benefit our lives if we attained unto more knowledge than anyone ever has, if we never used what we have learned to follow God better, or to help others? Solomon is a fine example of this. God made him the wisest man to ever walk the face of this earth. People came to him from around the known world to hear and learn from his wisdom, and God used Solomon in his early life in mighty ways. The nation of Israel was greatly blessed because of the wisdom of this single person. But late in life, Solomon became selfish and stopped using his great wisdom. In the Biblical understanding of wisdom and foolishness, he became one of the biggest fools that ever walked the earth! This happened because he stopped using his God-given wisdom for the spreading of the Truth and started using it to accumulate possessions and riches.

The Bible teaches us that we must put wise counsel into our lives, and that we must live by this counsel. We will become, next year, the people that we take counsel from this year! A person who seeks godly counsel will become a godly person. A person who takes the counsel of wicked men will become wicked, no matter what his background is. The godliest person on earth today can very quickly become the most wicked person on earth, and vice versa. It is of extreme importance to our Christian lives that we understand and take action upon this verse!

THE CRY OF WISDOM

Proverbs 8:1-3, 33, "Doth not wisdom cry? And understanding put forth her voice? She standeth in the top of high places, by the way in the places of the paths. She crieth at the gates, at the entry of the city, at the coming in at the doors... Hear instruction, and be wise, and refuse it not.

These verses tell us that wisdom cries out to mankind. She wants us to find her. She does not want to be hidden from anyone. She makes herself available to anyone that wants her. She promises blessings and riches to all that seek her out and follow her.

Why, then, is it so very hard for us to find wisdom? It is because we have allowed ourselves to be fooled into thinking that knowledge and wisdom are one and the same. We go to the best schools, learn new things, talk about all the things we know, how smart we are; and still fall in the same places over and over. Each time we fall, more of us is damaged; the foothold of sin becomes stronger, and life gets a little harder.

True wisdom is not found in schools. It is not found in old age. It is simply not to be found anywhere inside the realm of human knowledge alone. True wisdom is APPLIED KNOWLEDGE. If we know what is right, and refuse it, God says we are fools. If we know what is right and act upon it, we gain wisdom. Yes, we will stumble. We will fall. But each time we obey God in some area, we gain some wisdom.

Wisdom cries to us. God cries out for us to hear. "Hear instruction, and be wise, and refuse it not."

This, friend, is a crucial area for us if we want to grow stronger in the faith.

IN PURSUIT OF WISDOM: HOPE FOR THE SIMPLE

Proverbs 9:4-6, 10, "Whoso is simple, let him turn in hither: as for him that wanteth understanding, she saith to him, Come, eat of my bread, and drink of the wine which I have mingled. Forsake the foolish, and live; and go in the way of understanding… The fear of the LORD is the beginning of wisdom: and the knowledge of the holy is understanding."

Do you want wisdom? Do you want understanding? Do you deeply desire these things? If so, there is hope for you. Have you questioned why everything in your life fails, and why you can't change your life? The answer to this question is two-fold.

Yesterday, we saw that wisdom cries out to us. What, then, does she cry? She cries for the simple to simply come to her. Listen to her teachings, obey her lessons. She tells us that a man is shaped by the company he keeps. Iron sharpeneth iron, so a man sharpeneth the countenance of his friend. If we want to be wise, we must get rid of our foolish friends, and replace them with wise friends. We will never be any better than those we keep close to us. It is so important to have people in our lives that encourage us to do good, to do right.

These verses go on to tell us that wisdom begins with the fear of the Lord. This is not necessarily to be AFRAID of Him, but to have a healthy respect and awe for Him. If I respect someone, I do not want to disappoint them. I want to hear what they have to say. I want to follow their teaching. It means that I go to them for advice, and I cling to their every word.

The Lord wants to give us wisdom. He wants to throw blessings upon us. He will freely give us this wisdom and understanding. And with it, our lives will take on a whole different meaning. Where once was only found desperation and destruction now will be blessing and a life that glorifies God.

THE PROTECTOR

Matthew 12:20, "A bruised reed shall He not break, and smoking flax shall He not quench, till He send forth judgment unto victory."

This is such a small verse, and yet it perfectly sums up the personality and the life of Jesus Christ, and gives us such a great example of His love and His tenderness towards us. There is nothing more easily broken than a reed; just a tender piece of grass. And yet this verse goes as far as to say that He will not even break a piece that is almost broken already.

Back in Bible times, a shepherd would play music to keep his flock calm so they wouldn't get scared and scatter. This music was played from a type of flute, made from one of these reeds. The reeds grew almost everywhere, and the instruments were very quick and easy to make; they were also very easy to damage. Many were the times when the shepherd's instrument was damaged. It was much easier to throw it away and make a new one instead of fixing the damaged one.

Our verse goes on to say that a smoking flax shall He not quench. A smoking flax was a struggling, dying flame on a lamp wick that was running out of fuel. A lamp is obviously designed for one thing: to give light in times of darkness. A wick is what gives that light through fuel soaked from the reservoir of the lamp. But the lamp, as well as the wick, is useless without the fuel to keep the wick saturated so it can burn. As the flame dies down from lack of fuel, the cloth of the wick itself will start to burn, and slowly die out, but not before rendering damage to the wick, and much nasty, black smoke.

So how is this verse supposed to help us in times of trouble, hurt, or need? We can know for sure that we have a friend, even when all of our friends have forsaken us! We can be sure that we have a Savior tender and loving enough to protect us from the ones who would love to destroy us. When no one will listen or believe what we have to say, we can rest assured of the fact that He knows the truth. When we are damaged by circumstances or those who mean to do us harm, we have a Friend who will put His loving hands of protection around us and keep us from being broken. When our light is struggling to keep burning, He will never just extinguish it just because we are low on fuel. He will protect the struggling flame, add the fuel we so desperately need, and nurse it back into a strong light!

No matter where you are at in your walk, there will be many times when you will be this bruised reed that most people will just toss away. No matter how strong you are, there will be many times when you are surprised to find that your flame has suddenly started flickering and smoking. While many people find it much easier to just extinguish this burdensome flicker, the Savior will see very well that all it needs is a little help.

People are going to hurt you. You are going to get discouraged in life. You will face hardships in your life. You will be knocked down. Some of your closest friends in life will turn their backs on you. You are even going to make mistakes in your own life that will try to tear you apart. In every one of these things, you will not be strong enough to come through in your own power. It is the times like this that you can think of this verse, and remember the true lover of your soul;

the One who can, will, and does make all the difference in your life. He is the One constant, never changing One. He is the One true friend that will never leave or forsake you.

Put your trust in Him every day, especially those days that you can trust no one else. He will never do you wrong, and He will never finish the breaking of your bruised reed. He knows your deepest need, and He is very capable of providing it.

WHO OWNS MY STUFF?

Psalm 50:9-14, "I will take no bullock out of thy house, nor he goats out of thy folds. For every beast of the forest is mine, and the cattle upon a thousand hills. I know all the fowls of the mountains: and the wild beasts of the field are mine. If I were hungry, I would not tell thee: for the world is mine, and the fullness thereof. Will I eat the flesh of bulls, or drink the blood of goats? Offer unto God thanksgiving; and pay thy vows unto the most High."

Time after time, it seems that Christians catch themselves holding back things from the very God who has given them these things. We get concerned with the cares of this life, forgetting that our Heavenly Father is the ultimate provider for us. We hold back many things, including our love, our time, our money, and our talents. Often times we don't do these things out of spite, but out of fear.

We fear to give Him our whole heart in love, afraid of being hurt by Him, like we have been hurt by so many others. For many of us, this fear of hurt comes by much experience, and unfortunately, much of the hurt comes from those we have given our hearts to because they "are part of the Church." More of this hurt also comes from family and close friends.

We fear to give Him our time, because we know how precious time is, and how short it is. Our time is taken with work, responsibilities at home, care and maintenance of the things we possess. The thought of taking some of our precious time to give it to a God that we often know so little about is absurd to us.

We fear to give Him our money because this is something that is always in short supply. It takes so much money to live today, and we make so little of it. There are always things that need to be repaired, remolded, or replaced. We just don't see how we can afford to give to Him.

For most of us, the biggest fear of all is when we think of giving our talents to Him. God has gifted each of us in special ways, and these talents, many times, are the way we make our living. Some are good with their hands, but we fail to see how this could be used for God. Some are good with electronics, some with words, and many of us never realize our God-given talents, simply because we spend our lives in fear of trying to serve God.

God has an answer to each of these fears. For our fear of loving Him, He tells us in Matthew 12:28-30, "Come unto me, all ye that labour and are heavy laden, and I will give you rest. Take my yoke upon you, and learn of me; for I am meek and lowly in heart: and ye shall find rest unto your souls. For my yoke is easy, and my burden is light." It is only after we take the chance to love Him that we will see He is the only One who will never hurt us for any reason.

For our fear of giving Him our time, He says in Joel 2:25, " And I will restore to you the years that the locust hath eaten, the cankerworm, and the caterpillar, and the palmerworm, my great army which I sent among you." We foolishly refuse to lend Him our time on the basis that we don't have enough of it. He is the creator of time, and promises that if we serve Him, He will bless us for it.

172

For our fear of giving Him of our money, He says in Malachi 3:10, "Bring ye all the tithes into the storehouse, that there may be meat in Mine house, and put Me to the proof now herewith, saith the Lord of hosts, if I will not open to you the windows of heaven and pour you out a blessing, that there shall not be room enough to receive it." Again, we have to first "take a chance" on God; then He will show us the blessings.

And for our fear of giving Him our talents, He tells us in 1 Corinthians 4:7, " For who maketh thee to differ from another? And what hast thou that thou didst not receive? Now if thou didst receive it, why doest thou glory, as if thou hadst not received it?" God has given us the talents that we have to use for His glory.

Our Heavenly Father does not demand that we give to Him from the little that we have because He is greedy. He simply asks us to be willing to give all that we have, and once we make this step of faith, He is fully prepared and capable of giving back more than we have ever thought possible. You see, many Christians live in poverty, both physically and spiritually, simply because they are not willing to give to Him. And for many, they choose to continue to live in bondage to sin for the same reason. It is only when we are willing to give all that we have to Him that we will see His true healing power in every aspect of our lives.

One last thought: The US Government has over 17 billion dollars in unclaimed war bonds mostly from the WW2 era. These bonds have all matured, and are redeemable by the persons who hold the receipts. We would ask why in the world someone would not cash in on this great amount of wealth. But the same question should be asked by you and I. We know the God who holds all power and wealth, yet we hold back the little things we possess from Him. The answer is simple, and terrible, and completely our own faults: God's people have forgotten the God that we say we serve. Imagine the possibilities there would be for each of us, if we truly understood, and took advantage of, the promises God offers us.

THE SPIRIT OF POWER, LOVE, AND SOUND MIND

> 2 Timothy 1:7-8, "For God hath not given us the spirit of fear; but of power, and of love, and of a sound mind. Be not thou therefore ashamed of the testimony of our Lord, nor of me his prisoner: but be thou partaker of the afflictions of the Gospel according to the power of God."

Everyone is scared of something. Some people sit around worrying about things, and thinking up new stuff to worry about. Many people have phobias that are completely debilitating. Every day there seems to be something new to worry about: new ways to get sick; new powerful enemies; new laws making it harder to share our faith; the list is endless. And there are huge dangers of living in fear. The more we worry, the more health risks we face. The more we worry, the fewer opportunities we will take advantage of. If we are scared, we try to take actions that we think will keep us safe; many times making terrible choices that will affect our entire future. And lastly, it is when a person, or animal is scared that he becomes violent and aggressive.

Nothing good can come from living with a spirit of fear! This lifestyle will only cost us, as well as our friends and loved ones. It will cheapen our lives greatly, and will take us to an early grave. Our heavenly Father knows this, and throughout Scripture, try's to warn us of the foolishness of fearful existence.

Instead of living in fear, He has given us the recipe for powerful living. Best of all, it costs us nothing but the hindrance of being constantly fearful. Fear is ALWAYS caused by sin. If there were no sin in this world, there would be no reason to fear anything. Fear also always comes as a result of not being in a correct relationship with Jesus Christ. If we are in a good relationship with Him, we will have no reason to fear. You see, Jesus Christ has already taken the full cost of every sin you have ever committed. He has already paid the price; He has already beaten everything that sin could throw at Him. And He offers that victory to anyone who will take it!

And what a victory He offers! Instead of a spirit of fear, He offers power. The very power that we have been looking for to overcome our fears, He owns, and wants to give to us. Instead of fear, He offers love. This is the love that can only come from Jesus Christ; a love that overpowers the fear of personal harm or hardship placed upon us by our enemies. This love empowers us to live a life that will glorify Him in all things, showing those around us that He is real. Instead of fear, He offers a sound mind. Most of the things we worry about will never happen anyway. It comes from those two little life changing words, "what if." Jesus offers us a way to not remember the "what if's" of life, instead, focusing on living a life that will honor and glorify Him, no matter the consequences we might face. Once we know Him intimately, we know that not only has He already paid the price and made our fears meaningless, but He also controls the "what if's," allowing only those to get in that He wants to use in our lives for His glory.

And because of the new spirit He will install in us, we can go throughout life being unashamed of Him, His motives, His actions, and His love. Not only giving us the ability of living a life of power, love, sound mindedness, and being unashamed, He will allow us to look forward to being partakers of the hardships that will come because we are living our lives by and through His power. Although we will never look forward to pain and suffering, we will begin to understand that He will make all the hardships worthwhile in a day soon to come.

No one wants to hurt, but most of us understand by now that we will never live life on this earth without pain and suffering. Wouldn't it be so much better to live in His power and know that our pain and suffering from now on will be for His glory; and He will give us the strength to go through it?

THE GOOD SOLDIER OF CHRIST

2 Timothy 2:3-5, "Thou therefore endure hardness, as a good soldier of Jesus Christ. No man that warreth entangleth himself with the affairs of this life: that he may please Him who hath chosen him to be a soldier. And if a man also strive for masteries, yet is he not crowned, except he strive lawfully."

One thing we are absolutely guaranteed in our Christian life is that it will not be easy. The decision to follow Christ, trusting Him in faith for all we need, is not a decision to make lightly. Yet, it is the best decision that anyone will ever make. To make the best of it, there are many guidelines that Scripture gives us. In this passage we find a cornerstone that must be found in our lives if we wish to live victoriously.

The passage starts by telling us we must endure hardness to be a good soldier of Christ. The Christian will be faced with much hardness throughout his walk. We will find hardness from coworkers. If we are living the life we should be, our coworkers will know about our faith, and we will be made fun of. Another hardness we will find is from friends. Once we allow Jesus Christ to change our life, our old friends will find it harder and harder to come around us. Why? Because the things we used to love no longer hold us; we will instead hold fast to the Lord. One of the hardest hardnesses we will find is with family. Nothing hurts any more than to have family tell us they don't want us coming around anymore.

So why should we endure these things instead of just quietly living our life as a Christian? This passage goes on to say that we are in a war. This is very much a real war. A lot of it is fought on the battlefield of the mind and emotions, but it is a war, nonetheless. If we were in a physical war, we simply would never go across enemy lines to visit with the enemy that wants to see us defeated. We would do everything in our power to stay away from our enemy, and even to have the upper hand. We would want to have the best weapons, the best men operating those weapons; and we would want to be efficient in the use of as many of those weapons that we could be, because it is a matter of life and death for us! This passage gives us a vital key to the mastery of the weapons at hand.

This battle is fought in our minds. So what are the things that get us entangled? There are many different answers to this question, and they vary from person to person, from year to year, and many times from day to day. The best way to know what we have a chance of being entangled in is to just be aware of what is going on in our lives from day to day. Some easily become entangled in drugs; some in alcohol; some are entangled in bitterness and hate; for some it is nothing more than games or working; the list is endless! Whatever it is in our lives that is keeping us from honoring God is exactly what this passage is warning us about. But watch out, because it doesn't have to be bad things! If it is hindering our walk with Jesus Christ, even if it is not necessarily sinful, we have been entangled!

In the last sentence of this passage, we find something that may be even harder to keep right in our life. A true Christian wants to please God; this should be the biggest goal in our lives. But sometimes we get a goal set in our lives and think it is ok to use any means necessary to accomplish it. This is a lie from satan. The goals we have before us; the vision God has given us, must be accomplished lawfully. We cannot allow things to be done contrary to the Word of God, even if by doing so, we will be better equipped to serve God. What this sentence is saying is simple to see, but sometimes very hard to live out. If we are able to give huge amounts of money for God's work because we have been dishonest at work, God will not accept it from us! In our race, we must follow God's rule book!

Do you want God's blessing on your life? If so, these are two big areas to watch closely at all times. Do not entangle yourself with the cares of this world, and live your life in a manner that honors God's Law.

THE RIGHTEOUS WILL BE DELIVERED

Psalm 34:17-19, "The righteous cry, and the LORD heareth, and delivereth them out of all their troubles. The LORD is nigh unto them that are of a broken heart; and saveth such as be of a contrite spirit. Many are the afflictions of the righteous: but the LORD delivereth him out of them all."

This life is filled with sorrow and discouragement. It seems that every day the Christian deals with more stress, problems, and danger. If he fails to have a strong walk with the Lord, these things will pull him right out of any kind of a true Christian walk. And if he is in a strong and growing relationship with Christ, he had better make sure that personal time with his loving Savior stays at the top of his to do list. The walk of a true Christian will never be easy, but it has many priceless benefits during this life, as well as the next.

This passage tells us that the Lord hears every cry a Christian utters. Psalm 56 is a prayer King David prayed when he was captured by the Philistines in Gath. In verse eight, David says that God would put his tears in a bottle. King David was absolutely sure of the fact that God was present with him while he was going through this dangerous time of his life; not only present, but there to protect and keep him, while at the same time keeping record of the wrongs done against him. You can also be sure that whatever you are going through, God is there with you. He cares for you, and He wants to give you strength and wisdom to get through whatever it is you are facing.

Not only does the Lord hear the Christians cries during trouble, but He will also deliver them out of this trouble. Just as David was sure that the Lord would have His perfect will, no matter what his enemies wanted to do with him, you can know without a doubt that God is willing and able to deliver you during you times of need. God will never leave you to face your enemy alone, no matter what enemy you are facing in your life. He has a plan and a purpose for you, and also for the distress you are going through.

As always, the Scripture never gives empty promises, or promises without telling the seeker how to see said promises fulfilled in life. These promises are found in many passages throughout the Word of God, and testified to by many thousands of people, both in Bible times, and in our present day. You can have God's ear to hear you when you cry out, and His protection when you are faced with adversity, but there is a price you must pay.

Verse 18 of our text says the Lord is nigh unto them that are of a broken heart. The word nigh means that He is ready to hear you any time you cry out to Him. He is within reach any time you reach out in faith to Him, and He is ready to come to your rescue. The words "broken heart" mean someone who is humble towards Him; someone who realizes their need, their unworthiness of His affection and protection, their sinful heart, and their complete hopelessness without Him.

Many people today want God's blessings upon them. Many want God to deliver them out of trouble. Many want to talk of God's love and forgiveness. Few want to talk about what God wants from them in order give these great blessings. All that God promises, He is willing to provide, but these blessings are not guaranteed to those who will not humble themselves to Him.

The last verse in our text says that the righteous shall be troubled with many afflictions, but that God will deliver that righteous one out of them all. As in every aspect of the Christian walk, the wealth of these promises speak for themselves, but the choice to have them or reject them are yours, and yours alone. Will you humble yourself to the Lord today, asking Him to reveal even your hidden sins and cleanse your heart? James 4:8 says that if you will draw nigh to God, He will draw nigh to you. He wants to be your provider and your protection; He wants to be within your reach, but in order for this to happen, you must put yourself within His reach as well.

HIDING GOD'S WORD FOR A GREAT PURPOSE

Psalm 119:9-11, "Wherewithal shall a young man cleanse his way? By taking heed thereto according to Thy Word. With my whole heart have I sought thee: O let me not wander from Thy commandments. Thy Word have I hid in my heart, that I might not sin against Thee."

God's Word is a lamp for us to see by, the Word was from the beginning; not written by men, believers are sanctified by the Word of God, and the fact that every word of the Bible is true and eternal; we will be judged by God's Word. We understand that God is the Creator, and therefore He knows best when it comes to how we are supposed to live.

Our passage today begins by asking a simple, but very deep question; how is a person to cleanse his way? We each know from experience that when we try to do things ourselves, it ends up in chaos and destruction. The wonderful plans we have may work well in our minds, but when we try to implement them with our limited understanding, the end results can never be good. Many thousands of people have turned over a new leaf in life, trying to clean themselves up, only to find just as much trash and mold on the bottom of the leaf that was on the top. We cannot live lives worthy of God's love and favor! Isaiah 64:6, "But we are all as an unclean thing, and all our righteousnesses are as filthy rags; and we all do fade as a leaf; and our iniquities, like the wind, have taken us away." This verse tells us very plainly that there is nothing that comes from within us that will ever make us clean enough for us to have a relationship with God.

The Psalmist answers his question with the only acceptable solution for the problem. We are cleansed by taking heed to the Scriptures. The world tells us we are good enough like we are; God says the best we can do looks like filthy rags to Him. The devil tells us we can be like God; but God says we are fading away as a leaf. TV says we can find the answers within ourselves; God says we have been taken away by our iniquities. If we want to be in a right relationship with God, we must heed His Word, and let it make changes within us that can only come from the Holy Spirit.

The Psalmist goes on to say that he has sought God with his whole heart. God has become the most important thing in his life. Every day, his goal is to serve and please God, no matter what he faces. His prayer is that God will keep him from wandering away from God's presence. He knew he was prone to getting himself into sin, whatever the form may be. He knew his flesh would draw him away from God's love, before he even knew what may happening to him. He knew he had no power against the traps set against him by Satan. He knew his continued peace and rest in God depended upon God working in him, and for him. Friend, you and I must arrive at this same place if we ever want any hope of living a God-honoring life upon this earth.

Our passage ends with the key statement for any Christian who would desire to live a victorious life. "Thy Word have I hid in my heart, that I might not sin against Thee." You have heard that you should read your Bible every day. We should do that; but we should do so much more than just read it. There are countless people who grew up reading God's Word who died without ever knowing Him, or living a victorious life. What the Psalmist is talking about here goes much, much deeper than just spending a few minutes reading. You have also heard that you should memorize Scripture. This is also true; but memorizing alone will get you to the same place that only reading will do. We must do both of these things, but we must also take another step.

Hiding God's Word in our heart means to study, memorize, and meditate upon it. We must read it, but we must also take what we read with us throughout the day. We must think about it, asking God to show us the deeper meaning of the words we read and study. We must put it in the forefront of our hearts and minds throughout the day. We must let the Holy Spirit use its Words to change us, making us into what He wants us to be. We must let God lead us through Scripture, teaching us as we develop a closer walk with Him.

Friend, if you and I want to have a meaningful relationship with the Lord, we must let Him have His way in our lives. It is our choice; we can continue doing things the way we have always done them, and waste our prayers asking Him for victory over the sins we battle, or we can approach His Word as the final authority that it really is, letting Him change and mold us as He wants to, replacing the sins we struggle with, with His glorious presence in our lives. The only way to have true and lasting victory over sin is to replace that sin in our hearts with the living Word of God.

TRUE AND LASTING HEALING

Mark 2: 3-4, "And they come unto him, bringing one sick of the palsy, which was borne of four. And when they could not come nigh unto him for the press, they uncovered the roof where he was: and when they had broken it up, they let down the bed wherein the sick of the palsy lay."

In this story we see a group of people who were on a mission to see the Healer. They knew what they needed was a touch from the Master, and nothing was going to stand in their way. Whatever it took, they were willing to do. No cost was too great; no obstacle too large. And for their efforts, one that needed a miracle healing found just that.

In our day, there seems to be many ways to get where we want to go. If one way doesn't work well for us, we can just jump off the bus and try another way. It may be that it is too crowded. Or maybe that it means too much hard work. Maybe all of our friends are going a different way, but it looks to us that it is just about where we wanted to go, and we will just go with them. There is a "religion" that fits everyone out there somewhere. And don't they all go the same place anyway?

The hard truth for us to hear many times is that there is only one true Way. There is only one true Healer. There is only one true Helper. There is only One that can give us what we truly need for life. There are many paths we can take to make ourselves feel better about being who we are. There are many excuses that sound like real reasons that we can use for our failures. But if we want lasting change, change from the heart, there is only Jesus Christ that can give us what we need.

He is waiting for us to come to Him, but He will never force us to look to Him. He has the touch that we so desperately need, but will touch no person by force. His hands are capable of giving us true life; true healing; true freedom from the sins we are in bondage to. The real question for us is simple to ask, but needs a soul searching answer. How badly do we want His touch? How badly do we want healing in our hearts and relief from our bondage? Do we want it bad enough to leave the paths our friends and family are taking? Do we want it bad enough to walk alone to get it? Do we desire it enough to stop at nothing, whatever the price to ourselves? The path Jesus walked was a path filled with those who hated Him. If we follow Him, they will hate us also. But what we get in return will be eternally priceless!

RETURN TO THE FIRST WORKS

Revelation 2:2-4, "I know thy works, and thy labour, and thy patience, and how thou canst not bear them which are evil: and thou hast tried them which say they are apostles, and are not, and hast found them liars: And hast borne, and hast patience, and for my name's sake hast labored, and hast not fainted. Nevertheless I have somewhat against thee, because thou hast left thy first love. Remember therefore from whence thou art fallen, and repent, and do the first works; or else I will come unto thee quickly, and will remove thy candlestick out of his place, except thou repent."

As we look around today at a world that is dying, and a country that is dying, we must wonder to ourselves what went wrong. Never in the history of the world have things fallen apart so fast, and so thoroughly. The love and patriotism for our country that once filled the hearts of everyone here is gone, and has been replaced with hatred, or at best, apathy for what is in store for it.

Never in the history of our country has there been so many churches and religious organizations. One can find a program to help in any area he has a need or a desire in. One can find a church in almost any city or town, and quite possibly one that has any belief that he wants to believe. We are seeing a huge rise in religion in the world today, but still the world gets worse and worse. The answer to the question why can be found in the verses above.

Jesus told the Church of Ephesus that they had left their first love, and if they didn't repent and return to the first works, He was going to remove their candlestick out of its place. The choice was theirs to make: would they repent and follow God with their whole heart, giving Him the love and devotion He is due, or would they continue living the easy life, taking their stand against things for a purely selfish and prideful reason like they had started doing?

Friend, Jesus wants you to live a clean life today. Jesus wants you to work for Him, and to be a good person. But He wants you to do it for unselfish reasons. He wants your love and devotion to Him to be a priority in your life.

Remember when you were first saved? You wanted to tell everyone about the Lord. You couldn't wait to let your friends and family know what had happened to you. You were so excited about Jesus that you wanted to broadcast everywhere you went about His love and changing power, and you wanted to live a clean life because of your love for Him, not because it was something you are supposed to do. Jesus wants you to return to the first works, where your love for Him caused you to live for Him.

It is this love that is lacking in the world today! Religion is about rules and regulations; things you have to do, and things you cannot do. What Christ offers is so much more than this. He offers a relationship with the creator of the universe. He offers forgiveness to the sinner who has wronged Him, and also to the Christian who has known His love in the past, but forgotten it.

Just as the Church of Ephesus had a choice then, you have the same choice today. Just as the Church of Ephesus would face the consequences of their decisions then, you will face the same consequences. Jesus offers each Christian today forgiveness for a repentant heart, or destruction for a heart that has grown cold and callous toward Him. Which will you choose?

THE GOD OF NEW

Revelation 21:2-3, "And I saw a new heaven and a new earth: for the first heaven and the first earth were passed away; and there was no more sea. And I John saw the holy city, new Jerusalem, coming down from God out of heaven, prepared as a bride adorned for her husband."

Everything in and about this earth gets old and wears out. There is no exception to this rule. Our bodies age, become unhealthy, and die. Our clothes get old and thin. The houses we live in require maintenance continually because they are constructed from products that cannot withstand the damage radiated from the sun. Mankind is constantly designing things that they say are new and improved, will not wear out, run more efficiently, and withstand the damaging climate they will receive. But the one thing we can be sure about is the fact that nothing on this earth is eternal. Nothing will last forever. Eventually, it will wear out and cease to be useful.

Those who understand science know about a scientific law called "The Law of Entropy. A very basic explanation of this law is that there is a limited amount of energy in the universe. This amount of energy is constant, but each time it is used, it changes to a different form. This different form is always worth less than the previous form. In short, the very universe is winding down. Something started it, just like someone starts a spinning top. But the energy in the top winds down, and eventually the top stops spinning.

We can see this law's effects in everything around us, and in our own bodies. Each passing year, we find that our bodies can tolerate less and less strenuous activity, and we are more prone to failures and fractures. We can see it in the weather patterns that were once predictable, but now it seems that we have summer in winter time, and vice versa. We can see it in the horrendous diseases that mankind is getting everywhere, even from the time of birth.

Thankfully, our hope is not in this world, and not of this world! In our text, John tells us that he saw a new heaven and a new earth, because the old ones were passed away. Jesus meant what He said in John 14:3, when He said He was going to prepare a place for His disciples. It should be very encouraging for the Christian to know that this life is not all there is. As we see our bodies ageing and becoming weaker, it means that we are getting closer and closer to the bodies we will receive that will never age, grow weak, or become unhealthy!

Another key element in this passage is the fact that there is no sea on this new earth. The seas serve in this world as borders; something to keep the nations separated. At the end of time, when God makes the new earth, there will be no division among those who populate the earth. No more wars! No more strife between different races! The Creator God whom we serve is not a God of division, but a God of complete unity!

Don't get discouraged as you see another year passing by, and you see that you are getting older. As we age, we should also be becoming closer to our Savior, Jesus Christ. Don't get discouraged if the life you live today is one with very little comforts. This life should be just a warm up period for eternity! Don't let Satan fool you into living for this life. Everything in this world will soon be gone. Proverbs 11:24, "There is that scattereth, and yet increaseth; and there is that withholdeth more than is meet, but it tendeth to poverty." Live your temporary life today for the eternal life you will have tomorrow. The only things you will be able to keep in the next life are the things you give away in this one!

Friend, if you are living for this life, God says you cannot win. If you live with the attitude that this life is all there is, please heed the warning of God. This life is your only chance to establish a relationship with the Almighty God! If you waste this life, you will have wasted eternity.

God is a God of new. He offers a new, clean life to you, in exchange for the one that sin has destroyed.

IN TIMES OF ADVERSITY: MORE PRECIOUS THAN GOLD

1 Peter 1:5-9, "Who are kept by the power of God through faith unto salvation ready to be revealed in the last time. Wherein ye greatly rejoice, though now for a season, if need by, ye are in heaviness through manifold temptations: that the trial of your faith, being much more precious than of gold that perisheth, though it be tried with fire, might be found unto praise and honour and glory at the appearing of Jesus Christ: whom having not seen, ye love; in whom, though now ye see Him not, yet believing, ye rejoice with joy unspeakable and full of glory: receiving the end of your faith, even the salvation of your souls."

This is such a thought-provoking passage that we can meditate on at times of great trials in our lives. We have assurance through God's Word that we are kept by His power, not ours, to salvation. The faith we put in Him is all we need to be assured of this wonderful fact! This alone is enough to keep us rejoicing, no matter what tribulation we must go through in this lifetime. Though it may hurt and cost us much in this life, we are assured that any pain we face today will be well worth any cost, in the very near future.

We all know very well how precious gold is today. Each day, gold is worth more and more. The value of our dollar may fluctuate, but if we have precious metals, we know their value is a constant. But this passage is telling us that the trials and tribulations we go through in this life are worth so much more to God than all the gold we could ever give Him. The manifold, or many and continuous temptations and trials we go through add daily to God's estimation of the worth of us, as His children.

The trials of this life have an eternal value for the Christian. Each trial we face, and through God's power, overcome, makes our salvation sweeter to us. Each hardship we endure draws us closer to our Savior. Each battle with our enemy allows us to see just another way that God can have victory in our lives even when we are facing a hopeless situation. Each hurt we have thrown at us only allows us to learn of another aspect of godly peace and contentment, which can only come by the very trials of our faith that we cringe to think about coming our way. God grows us spiritually through these times in our lives!

Even when we can't see the good in the trial we are facing, God has allowed it for this purpose. Our job is to cling to Him, His love, and His promises. The gold this world cherishes, and is willing to kill and maim for will soon perish. The power those who harm others for will soon cease to exist. The lies and deception that have helped so many into prosperous and powerful places in this world will soon be revealed. The world may look today at the Christian, mocking and laughing at what it calls an ignorant faith, but there is coming a day very soon when the Creator of this universe will reveal just how the faith you practice has helped you to know the one Person who can truly help you when you need it most.

Our passage goes on to say that the trial of our faith will be found unto praise and honor and glory at the appearing of Jesus Christ. Throughout this life, the Christian will find very little praise, honor, and glory. We must understand that we are not living for this world and what it can offer. Everything it has will soon vanish away, as will this life we live here. The greatest glory that can be found will be found as we come face to face with our Savior, Jesus Christ! It is then that we will fully understand answers to our trials and tribulations upon this earth. It is then that we will understand what true life really means. It is then that we will be able to fully appreciate the hardships we once faced in this lifetime; because we will understand that it was those hardships that made us cling ever so much more to our Savior.

"Receiving the end of your faith, even the salvation of your souls." Don't lose hope; don't give up the Christian walk, because of the trials and temptations you may face today. Satan wants to use them to destroy and discourage; God wants to use them to make heaven sweeter to you. Rest in God. Give Him your troubles and worries, and trust Him to make your life worth living, and to give it meaning.

IN TIMES OF ADVERSITY: JOY THROUGH TEMPTATION

James 1:2-4, "My brethren, count it all joy when ye fall into divers temptations; knowing this, that the trying of your faith worketh patience. But let patience have her perfect work, that ye may be perfect and entire, wanting nothing."

How is it possible to remain joyful even when going through these times of life where we struggle, wondering if we are going to make it through this particular part of life? Why is it that God will not just take us around these temptations and trials that we face? Wouldn't it be better for His work if He would ensure that His children never had a chance to fall into temptations or trials, and make the wrong choices?

If we look at these questions strictly from a human standpoint, with our limited knowledge and wisdom, the answer would be that it would be much better for God to keep us from these things. But we must remember that God sees, thinks, and knows much deeper and farther than we do. He certainly has the power to ensure that nothing bad ever touches us. But He has chosen to allow each person who has ever lived to have free will in the decisions they make. Because each person has free will, we can also be sure that some of the terrible choices that we make will affect others in our world, and the ones they make will affect us in our world as well. God, in His wisdom, grace, and mercy, allows these things to happen.

Another thing we must remember as we walk through this imperfect life is that there are many things that God does protect us from. These things, many times, are things that we know nothing about, but God knew that they would ruin us, and has protected us from them. We who are former addicts, we can undoubtedly understand that God has looked down upon us with huge amounts of grace and mercy, and delivered us from problems that we can only blame ourselves for ever having been involved in. We can and should be very thankful and joyful as we look at these two things!

Lastly, we should be thankful to God for allowing us to go through the trials and temptations that He allows us to go through because we understand through Scripture that He has a building process planned for our lives, and these things, many times, are engineered directly by God Himself. He allows these temptations and trials to come our way because He wants us to learn from them. He wants us to stay close to Him, and as we run into trouble, He knows that we will come to Him for help and answers again and again.

Although many times we must endure terrible things at the hands of our enemy, we are instructed to count it all joy. These things, either brought to us by the hand of God himself, or allowed by God to get through His invincible protection, are allowed to us for our ultimate benefit, and the benefit of those around us that He wants to impact through our lives!

We should never get frustrated or angry with God when going through these troubling times. We need to thank Him for His love, and for being willing to teach and train us to be better and stronger Christians, and understand that through His wisdom, this is the way He is instructing us today.

The trying of our faith, when we face it correctly, asking Him for wisdom to make the correct decisions, is working and strengthening our patience. Today, when facing these things, let God remind you that it is through this process that you are developed into the person that God wants you to be tomorrow. Nothing that happens to you today will happen by chance. Nothing that comes to you today is going to catch your Savior by surprise. He is maturing you and teaching you things today that you will need for your spiritual survival tomorrow. Let Him work on you. Rest in Him, and never let your faith waiver. He has your best interest in mind!

IN TIMES OF ADVERSITY: JUST TRUST

Proverbs 3:5-6, "Trust in the LORD with all thine heart; and lean not unto thine own understanding. In all thy ways acknowledge Him, and He shall direct thy paths."

We love to read verses like this when everything is going great for us. It is so wonderful to give praise and glory to the Lord for the times when He is answering our prayers the way we want Him to answer them. We can stand and tell those around us of His love and grace to us as He keeps the enemy well away from us. We feel fabulously Christian when we are walking the beautiful, sunny mountaintop. We love to tell others how He blesses us when we are happy with the things He has brought into our lives.

But what about those times when everything coming at us seems to be against us, and we feel as though we are trying to swim upstream against a current that is just too powerful. We no sooner take a step forward, and then something comes along and knocks us two steps back. What about those times when we feel as though we cannot even reach heaven with a prayer, let alone have a prayer be answered? What about those times we can feel our enemy breathing down the back of our necks, feel his hands wrap around our dreams, and watch as he destroys what we have been laboring for, and dreaming about for so very long?

It is in these times of great pain and adversity that we not only do not feel like Christians, but the world around us seems to call out to us to give up on the God we have entrusted our lives to. It is during these times that your enemy can be heard most clearly in your mind, telling you that the Savior you have chosen to follow is a liar. This whisper is given by the father of lies himself. This whisper is given by the one who lives for the destruction of your life.

My friend, it is in these times that you need to trust God more than you have ever trusted Him before! Though you may not understand why God allows these things to happen in your life, and you may never know why they happen, you can be sure that He has a purpose in allowing you to face these things. Isaiah 55:8-9, "For my thoughts are not your thoughts, neither are your ways My ways, saith the LORD. For as the heavens are higher than the earth, so are My ways higher than your ways, and My thoughts than your thoughts." God sees things very much clearer than you and I can ever see them. We see what is happening today, but God sees your life in its entirety as He looks down at you today. He knows what you will need to know next week, next month, and next year. He knows where you will be serving Him in the future, and He knows how to prepare you today, so that He can place you where He wants you, as a mature and effective servant to Him.

Your mind may tell you that things are falling apart in your life, but God sees that if you will just trust in Him, things are not falling apart; they are simply falling into place. It is often necessary for progress that things are moved around, destroyed, or replaced. Your spiritual life is no different. There are things in your life that God cannot use. There are things that, if He allowed them to stay, would hinder His plan for you. The movement, replacement, and destruction of these things will always be painful for the Christian, but if they are not taken care of, the Christian will cease to grow, and will never be useful to the Savior.

If you find, as you go out today, that God has chosen to rebuild something in your life, give Him full access to the things He must destroy. He is the Master Builder, and will never make a mistake in this building process! Though your mind will tell you to run away, or to cling on to something that God says must go, He is asking you to trust Him with your life. Don't let your small and incomplete understanding get in the way of His ultimate knowledge. Trust Him with your whole heart; your whole being; and with everything that you hold near and dear to your heart! Even when He points you in a direction that you do not understand, He promises that if you will just submit to Him in all areas, and with all things, He will direct you in the path that is best!

IN TIMES OF ADVERSITY: SECRET REST

Psalm 91:1-3, "He that dwelleth in the secret place of the most High shall abide under the shadow of the Almighty. I will say of the LORD, He is my refuge and my fortress: my God; in Him will I trust. Surely He shall deliver thee from the snare of the fowler, and from the noisome pestilence."

There are many times the Christian finds himself in situations that look hopeless. As he looks at the problems he faces in life, there is no place to run and hide from his afflictions. Any direction he chooses looks like it is the wrong choice. It is in these times that God's promises are so comforting to us.

If we study the life of Job, we can see that terrible things happened to Job, and there was no apparent reason for them. Often, when adversity comes to us, it is because God is trying to get our attention about some area in our lives that is displeasing to Him. Sometimes, though, He allows this adversity simply to grow our faith, or draw us ever closer to Him. It is vital to the Christian that he is constantly searching and seeking a closer relationship with Christ, and when these afflictions come to him, that he turns to, instead of away from, the Lord.

Our verse tells us that he that dwelleth in the secret place shall abide under the shadow of the Almighty. God doesn't want us to only run to Him on the days we wake up with problems. God wants His people to dwell, or live, in this secret place. The benefits for making this our dwelling place is that we will be in His shadow.

On even the hottest summer days, when the sun is baking down on us, when a cloud comes between us and the sun, we can feel an immediate decrease in temperature. An added bonus we often feel is the cool breeze upon our faces. The heat that was upon us only moments ago is still there, but there has been a reprieve in the intensity.

The same thing is spiritually true for the Christian that makes his dwelling place in the secret place of the most High. The enemy is out there every second of the day, looking for a way to destroy a Christian testimony, or family. We can be sure that he never sleeps, and will pass up no chance to create havoc in our lives. But we have a way out, even where there seems to be none.

If you and I will dwell in the secret place, we will have a barrier that no enemy can cross to get to us. In the midst of troubles and worries, trials and struggles, and enemies who want to see us destroyed, we can have the shadow of the Almighty God between us and all trouble, keeping us well out of the reach of these destroyers.

Verse two says that the Lord is a refuge. In the Old Testament times, there were cities of Refuge where those who were guilty of crimes punishable by death could flee to for protection from those who could legally pass sentence upon them. By God's law, if these people remained inside the walls of these cities of Refuge, no harm could come to them, even from those who had a right to do them damage. God provides Himself as a city of refuge for the believer who would purpose in their hearts to dwell with him.

Next, our verse says that the Lord is a fortress. Criminals prey upon property that is left unprotected. There are so many houses where people think their things are protected, that are broken into and everything is taken, and our spiritual lives are no different. If we have our spiritual possessions unsecured, the enemy will destroy all that we think that we have. God is this fortress! Nothing can get through His defenses! If we are dwelling with Him, we will be safe from the things that want to destroy and maim.

Verse three says that He will deliver us from the snare of the fowler. Satan lays these snares for us throughout our life, and in many areas where we would never suspect. Once in the snare, it is impossible for one to find his way out. These snares are designed to entrap those who would dwell in this secret place, placed just outside of the protective hand of God. As soon as we make the mistake of thinking we can spend just a little time outside of the presence of God, we will be entangled. God can, and will, protect His children from these snares that will ruin our lives.

We are weak people, and simply cannot fend for ourselves in this world filled with enemies. But God offers His protection to us, if we will simply commit to dwell within His presence. Though He will not stop the storms from coming, He will be a shadow. Though the enemy may rage, and the criminal come to destroy, He will be our safe city. Though the snares of this world are set for us, He will guide our steps around them.

Are you dwelling in the secret place today?

IN TIMES OF ADVERSITY: THE LOVE OF GOD

Romans 8:36-39, "As it is written, for Thy sake we are killed all the day long; we are accounted as sheep for the slaughter. Nay, in all these things we are more than conquerors through Him that loved us. For I am persuaded, that neither death, nor life, nor angels, nor principalities, nor powers, nor things present, nor things to come, Nor height, nor depth, nor any other creature, shall be able to separate us from the love of God, which is in Christ Jesus our Lord."

This world has a way of finding our weaknesses and hammering on them. It can find a very small flaw in our defensive armor, and within a very short amount of time turn that small flaw into something that so large, at least in our own eyes, that we can see nothing else. The world can find the cracks in our Christian walk and turn them into an unpassable grand canyon in our lives. This is the world we live in; this is the enemy we have.

Satan abhors to see the Christian progressing in a godly life that glorifies the Savior. He will go to any length to either destroy you, or discourage you in your walk. He will bring your past life back to your mind, accusing you of being a fake. He will bring back your old friends, reminding you of the life you once lived, trying to make you ashamed of what you try to live now. He is a very strong adversary; one that you cannot beat! He will do anything to get between you and your Savior.

As a Christian, you must never forget your past. But more importantly, you must never forget the power and faithfulness of the One who traded His life so that you may know true life. Jesus Christ was willing to give away all of His glory and honor to come to make a way that you might share His life. And if He was willing to give up all this, you can be sure that He is willing to fight the battles that you cannot win.

Our passage tells us that, even though we face a hateful foe in a powerful world, we cannot lose the battles we face, because Christ has already won the victory for every one of them. Jesus Christ has defeated the one that wanted to destroy Him, and He has defeated him so that you and I can have victory in this life, even with our weaknesses, flawed armor, and grand canyons of sin and past failures.

Don't let Satan steal the victory that Christ has won for you. He brings your past back to you because he wants you to wallow in the shame of your previous lifestyle; but God lets this happen so that you might continue to see your need for Him. Satan brings your old friends to you to try to lure you back into the life that you once thought was fun; Christ allows them to come to you so that He might love them to Himself through your life. Satan seeks your destruction, even through Christian friends who have lost their way; Christ wants to witness to them of His love, forgiveness, and healing power through your life.

Christ wants to remind you daily, that though you face adversity and pain every day you will live for Him, that He has the power to get you through any situation that may arise. The sins you battle can only be defeated through His power. Those who may hate you and tell lies to or about you are not truly your enemies, but are being used by your true enemy to derail you, and set you back in your walk. No matter what you may face today, Jesus Christ wants you to remember His love for you. Neither death, nor life, nor angels, nor principalities, now powers, nor things present, nor things to come, nor height, nor depth, nor any other creature, shall be able to separate you from the love of God, which is in Christ Jesus your lord.

What else can come after you today? These verses cover anything that you could possible find yourself in a battle with! Jesus Christ has it covered. All He asks from you is your love and commitment in return. Will you remember Him today? Will you love Him, because He has loved you? Will you live for Him, because He has died for you? Don't forget your past, but let the Lord Jesus use it for His glory and honor. Let Him shine through your life today!

THE HEALER

I came to my Lord with a heavy heart,
It seemed that my world was being torn apart.
As I looked at my life, I began to question;
My faith, my God, in desperation.

My friends had departed, their promises disregarded,
They'd all found a new road to travel
My dreams had all vanished, and all my hope had been banished
My goals were too far, and unraveled.

For years I had struggled, time and plans had been juggled,
The goal of my life was to be
In touch with my Maker, my God and my Savior,
In use by His hand as a key.

As the years had gone by, with a few hopes to try,
They had all been found delusive.
Then I thought I had come to a place in my life,
That all of those failed hopes could be

For a while it seemed, that the things I had dreamed
Were all falling in place like a tee
There were friends, jobs and plans
There was training, and even a degree
Although very busy, my life had become carefree.

The dreams got bigger, the jobs came with rigger
The friends began to show their true color.
The help I once had, of a sudden came unclad
Once again, I began to reconsider.

I decided to give up; refuse to drink from this cup
I was sick of my plans going awry.
I would do my own thing, I would be my own man
Start doing something that came with a pension plan.

Oh, love of my Savior, who did me the favor
Of showing me His grace, His mercy, and His patience
In my years of doubt, He gave just enough drought
To keep me from being---another victim of the depraver.

Quietly He began, to show me His plan
His love, honor and faithfulness, to make me a man
Has been years in the making, my heart being ground for retaking
He simply waits for my waking.

The trials I've faced, and the way I have raced
Is not a testament to His wonderful plan
But He wants to use the trials and lessons I've seen
To make me a godly man.

Printed in the United States
By Bookmasters